The National Poetry Series established the Robert Fagles Translation Prize in 2007. This award is given annually to a translator who has shown exceptional skill in the translation of contemporary international poetry into English.

The Robert Fagles Translation Prize
2007

Marilyn Hacker,
King of a Hundred Horsemen

A translation from the French of
Roi des cent cavaliers
by Marie Étienne

Selected by Robert Hass

The National Poetry Series was established in 1978 to ensure the publication of five poetry books annually through participating publishers. Publication is funded by the Lannan Foundation, Stephen Graham, Joyce & Seward Johnson Foundation, Glenn and Renee Schaeffer, Juliet Lea Hillman Simonds Foundation, the Tiny Tiger Foundation, and Charles B. Wright III.

Also by Marie Étienne

POETRY

Blanc clos
Le Point d'aveuglement
La Longe
Lettres d'Idumée
Le Sang du guetteur
Les Barbares
La Face et le lointain
Katana
Anatolie
Roi des cent cavaliers
Dormans

ESSAY

Antoine Vitez, professeur au
    Conservatoire

"LES COULOIRS DE LA PROSE"
(between prose and poetry)

Eloge de la rupture
Les Passants intérieurs
Les Soupirants

NOVELS

Clémence
Antoine Vitez, le roman du théâtre
Sensō, la guerre
L'Inconnue de la Loire
L'Enfant et le soldat

Also by Marilyn Hacker

POETRY

Presentation Piece
Separations
Taking Notice
Assumptions
Love, Death and the Changing of the
    Seasons
Going Back to the River
Selected Poems
Winter Numbers
Squares and Courtyards
First Cities: Collected Early Poems
Desesperanto
Essays on Departure: New and
    Selected Poems

TRANSLATIONS

Edge (poems by Claire Malroux)
A Long-Gone Sun (poem-narrative
    by Claire Malroux)
Here There Was Once a County
    (poems by Vénus Khoury-Ghata)
She Says (poems by Vénus Khoury-
    Ghata)
Birds and Bison (poems by Claire
    Malroux)
Last News of Mister Nobody (poems
    by Emmanuel Moses)
A House at the Edge of Tears (a novel
    by Vénus Khoury-Ghata)
Poème et Peinture: Poem and Painting
    (poems by Dominique de
    Villepin)
Charlestown Blues (poems by Guy
    Goffette)
Nettles (poems by Vénus Khoury-
    Ghata)

KING OF A
HUNDRED HORSEMEN

MARIE ÉTIENNE

KING OF A
HUNDRED HORSEMEN

TRANSLATED FROM THE FRENCH BY
MARILYN HACKER

FARRAR, STRAUS AND GIROUX
NEW YORK

Farrar, Straus and Giroux
18 West 18th Street, New York 10011

Distributed in Canada by Douglas & McIntyre Ltd.
Printed in the United States of America
Originally published in 2002 by Flammarion, France, as *Roi des cent cavaliers*
Published in the United States by Farrar, Straus and Giroux
First American edition, 2008

Grateful acknowledgment is made to the following publications, in which
parts of this book first appeared: *Babel*, the online journal of the
International Cities of Rescue program ("War Diary"); *Crazyhorse* ("Ocean /
Emotion"); *Mantis* ("War Diary"); *New Letters* ("The End and the
Beginning"); *Pleiades* ("Some of Them Are Japanese"); *PN Review*, UK
("Ocean / Emotion"); *Poetry Review*, UK (sections 24, 25, 32, 33, 68, 70, 72,
73, 74, 77, 90, 92, 93, 94, and 99); *Studio*, the online journal ("Proof by the
Birds"); and *WordsWithoutBorders*, the online journal ("A Witness
Disappears").

Poems of Marie Étienne's translated by Marilyn Hacker not in this book
appear in *The Yale Anthology of Twentieth-Century French Poetry* (Yale
University Press, 2004) and in *New European Poets* (Graywolf Press, 2008).

Library of Congress Cataloging-in-Publication Data
Étienne, Marie.
  [Roi des cent cavaliers. English]
  King of a hundred horsemen / Marie Étienne ; translated from the
French and with a preface by Marilyn Hacker.
    p.   cm.
  ISBN-13: 978-0-374-18118-5 (hardcover : alk. paper)
  ISBN-10: 0-374-18118-7 (hardcover : alk. paper)
  I. Hacker, Marilyn, 1942–   II. Title.   III. Title: King of 100 horsemen.

PQ2665.T49R6513 2008
843'.914—dc22

                                                        2008013847

Designed by Ralph Fowler / rlf design

www.fsgbooks.com

10 9 8 7 6 5 4 3 2 1

Contents

Translator's Preface

Marie Étienne, born in Menton in the Alpes-Maritimes, spent her childhood in Indochina, in what is now Vietnam, during the Second World War and the beginning of the Viet Minh struggle for independence: her father was a French military officer who survived capture by the Japanese. These origins (as well as her father's prison journals) are the basis of her 2002 novel *Sensō: La guerre*, a kaleidoscopic impression of the war and the multiple displacements of a child between cultures, and of her 2007 memoir/fiction *L'Enfant et le soldat*. Her own education continued in France and in Dakar, and she has remained a traveler and an ambassador between literary cultures all her life.

Many prominent French poets, young, less young, "experimental" and "established," have in common, in the shadow of Mallarmé, not merely the aim of extreme concision but a conscious thrust to banish narrativity from their work: these seem to be the poets who have come to represent French poetry to Anglophones. But there are other currents and countermeasures. There is a certain lyricism unabashedly claiming Verlaine's heritage; there is the virtuoso use of invented or inherited constraints by the Oulipo poets, constraints that paradoxically induce narrative or its semblance; there are the variously broad strokes and wide linguistic horizons of vastly different Francophone poets of African, Arabic, French Canadian, or West Indian heritage whose work is more and more appreciated in France; there are poets incorporating argot, quotidian speech, and street speech with gusto into their work. Marie Étienne, omnivorous reader though she is, cannot easily be placed in any "movement": her work seems sui generis, and this perhaps has to do with the hybridity of her literary origins, both her expatriate childhood and what followed.

From 1979 to 1988, Marie Étienne worked as assistant to the innovative French theater director Antoine Vitez, whose courses on the theater she had followed as part of her doctoral thesis research, at the Théâtre d'Ivry and the Théâtre National de Chaillot. Commuting to Paris from a different life in Orléans with a husband and young daughter, her responsibilities included the organization of Monday evening poetry readings that took place on the sets of the theater pieces performed on the other evenings of the week. Étienne was then a well-published "emerging" writer and a frequent contributor to the lively, long-lived, and politically engaged quarterly *Action Poétique*, well placed to integrate poetry-off-the-page into the life of the theater. It was a heady period in French literary life, as it was in the poet's own development, during which *Action Poétique* enjoyed the collaboration of such varied figures as the poet/novelist/mathematician Jacques Roubaud and the Lacanian historian-journalist Elizabeth Roudinesco. The contributions of aesthetic and political radicals in the arts seemed to be welcome. Vitez, as befits a director of Racine and Molière (and as another artist seeking further integration of disciplines), saw poetry and theater on a continuum. But Étienne was also a chronicler of the daily life of the theater troupe: interactions among actors, stage managers, and the director; the challenges posed by the troupe's physical settings; the pauses and separations (holidays, departures to perform in repertory) which brought the participants back together with renewed energy, increased impatience, or both. More than Vitez's amanuensis, she was one of his privileged interlocutors, his Boswell and dramaturge. She recorded in a series of notebooks different aspects of their multiform collaboration: Vitez's written and spoken reflections, her own reactions to the plays and their mise-en-scène, the momentous shift from a bare-bones community theater in Ivry to the monumental Théâtre de Chaillot at the Trocadéro. Vitez's work combined a commitment to the classics with a passionate engagement in socially progressive causes during the years of the student uprisings in France and the Algerian independence movement that put an end to the French colonial presence. Vitez reinterpreted the classics—Greek tragedy in particular, but also the French classics—in the light of current events, and his vision extended to his instruction and direction of young actors at the Conservatoire d'Art Dramatique and the École de Chaillot.

Marie Étienne's collaboration with Vitez followed a five-year period in her life when theater and poetry were the joint subjects of her concentration. Her theatrical engagement was coeval with her attaining greater notice, indeed, with her growing confident self-definition as a writer, which the director—known in a different discipline but actively interested in contemporary poetry—was one of many established figures to encourage. Like plants burgeoning in another part of a garden, her own early books were beginning to appear at this time. Étienne's engagement with poetry (and narrative prose), in part because of the interactive and theatrical context of its development, encompassed from the start the possibility of a polyvocal text, of language as a cue in a choreography of real or imagined motion, of writing that engages in dialogue with other texts, other cultures, other disciplines, incorporating "spoken" dialogue itself into poetry in a way most contemporary French poets have eschewed. The synthesis of the contemporary and the classical, of the tragic and the mundane, of the quotidian transformed by the prisms of myth and history, is present in Marie Étienne's poetry. So is a theatrical framework of invented fixed forms for snatches of narrative that veer from the seemingly ordinary to the surreal, from the urban present to an oneiric time-beyond-time. Several of the sequences in the present book draw on the theater, play with its rituals, utilize dialogue in place of or superseding narration, put the stage itself on stage. The ludic and the surreal have always played an important part in Étienne's work, from her debut as a writer. She has kept a lively if distanced or bemused interest in the Oulipo movement, in which her *Action Poétique* colleague Jacques Roubaud remains a signal figure. She herself is interested more in a philosophical reflection on the direction taken by written texts as they develop than in a "submission," however playful or arbitrary, to form or formula. For her the writer is the "coachman driving the team of horses pulling the carriage," exercising a control kept by awareness of a constant and fruitful tension between the conscious and the unconscious, as well as between content and form.

Marie Étienne now lives in Paris, where she is a frequent contributor to literary and book review journals, in particular the literary critical journal *La Quinzaine littéraire*, for which she has written regularly since 1985, reviewing fiction, literary nonfiction, and poetry. For several years, she wrote a monthly page for the journal *Aujourd'hui Poème*, which she often used to present contemporary foreign poetry in translation to its readership. She has been especially instrumental in bringing the work of Vietnamese and Japanese poets to a French audience.

Étienne is at present the author of eleven books of poems and nine books of prose, which could be variously classed as fiction, memoir, and cultural history, some partaking of all three. She has edited and introduced two anthologies of contemporary poetry. Her work with Vitez, including transcriptions of her notebooks of the era, resulted in *Antoine Vitez: le roman du théâtre*, a book in a genre Americans would call literary memoir, published in 2000, a decade after the director's death and almost twenty years after their collaboration. It offers an invaluable aperçu of a collaborative artistic endeavor and a signal era in contemporary French theater. Other recent books include the novel *L'Inconnue de la Loire* (2004); *Les Passants intérieurs*, an experimental prose work (2004); *Les Soupirants* (2005), short narratives which upend and parody the expectations of literary pornography; *Dormans*, a book of poetry (2006); and *L'Enfant et le soldat*, an autobiographical novel also published in 2006.

The "condition of women," and a subversion of received thought on that subject, is a subtext in more than one of Marie Étienne's books, though rarely is it presented in the context of autobiographical material. Rather, it is implied in the account of a soldier's wife's life in Indochina in the 1940s, or of the narrow horizons facing a young girl in the prewar French provinces in the novels drawing on her family history. The troublesome connection of a credible woman's persona with the erotics of a Bataille, a Breton, or a Jouve is indicated in the surreal fiction of *Les Soupirants*. An early sequence drawing directly on the poet's theatrical experience is a series of prose-poem letters in the spirit of Ovid's *Héroides*, written in the persona of Racine's Bérénice exiled in Iduméa to the imperial Roman lover who banished her. The lyric "I" in Marie Étienne's poetry is a protean, not to say unreliable narrator, an inveterate storyteller, a speaker constantly subverting the very expectations of the poem in its contemporary guises, yet it (or "she") reasserts just as persistently the possibility of such an "I" having a voice marked as a woman's while engaged in quests and exploration rather than self-examination: the explorer's/travel narrative is one of the many "forms" borrowed and transfigured by the poet.

Although the consideration of women's poetry/women's writing *as such* is somewhat alien to many French women writers (at least those not associated with the "*Psychanalyse et politique*" movement, who themselves disavow the term "feminist"), Étienne did a considerable study of twentieth-century French women poets for a chapter on the subject in the 2003 anthology *Beyond French Feminisms*. One of her discoveries perusing anthologies was exactly that of the American feminist writer Joanna Russ in her own assessment of canonical English anthologies published before 1980: there was a uniform, modest percentage of women poets included, but, while the presence of individual male poets was constant from one anthology to the next, those women included would disappear and be replaced within the persistent 5 to 10 percent. Women poets' place in contemporary French poetry is still an uneasy one, as compared with Anglophone poetry, and also with Francophone Canadian poetry, where their highly significant role in the creation of a specifically Canadian modernism is universally acknowledged. Fourteen women, Canadians and other non-French Francophones included, figure in the 2000 edition of the 670-page Gallimard pocket anthology of French poetry of the second half of the twentieth-century, containing work by 150 poets born between 1907 and 1950 (with only two women born in the last decade of this time span). This can be contrasted with a considerable presence of women fiction writers and literary essayists in every register from the detective novel to all flavors of avant-garde. Given the exaggerated care with which the editorial borders seem to be guarded, it is paradoxical that in France, poetry itself has suffered even greater critical segregation and exclusion—in the literary press, on bookshop and library shelves—than it has in the United States. Nor is it alternatively propagated and disseminated by well-attended public readings. This might well constitute an additional reason for a writer, a woman writer in particular, to prefer not to confine or define herself by a single literary genre.

Marie Étienne has always composed poetry and prose alternately or simultaneously, seeing the genre barrier as arbitrary in many instances. In an extended essay in a recent issue of the journal *Formes poétiques contemporaines*, she examined the prose poem as genre, with its attractions and pitfalls, and scrutinized its uses by a variety of contemporaries. She resists the idea of a "collection" of poems, seeing in each book of her poetry as much unity as in a work of fiction, and concomitantly regards some of her fiction as approaching the long poem in prose. Indeed, "fiction" is as limiting a definition of her work in prose as "collection" might be of her carefully constructed poetic works. Some of these books could more properly be called extended memoir than novels: extended, that is, into an individual or familial past, but with an elaboration that has more to do with acknowledged imagination and linguistic invention than with documentary reconstruction. This is a genre that readers of contemporary French writing will associate with (for example) Marguerite Duras, who shared, albeit in a different generation, Marie Étienne's experience of a Southeast Asian childhood, and with Marguerite Yourcenar's nonfiction re-creations of her maternal and paternal family histories, which partake necessarily of the fictional; but also with the contemporary work of writers as divergent as Patrick Modiano, Richard Millet, Hervé Guibert, Leïla Sebbar, and Hélène Cixous. Other books of Étienne's make use of formal experimentation in a stylized and elegant manner that has little to do with the depiction of a presumed reality. Both the Prix Mallarmé–winning *Anatolie* and the recent *Dormans*, unified books labeled "poetry," alternate verse, including rhymed short-lined quatrains and decasyllabic dixains (a form associated with the metaphysical-erotic "blasons" of Maurice Scève), with pages of prose narrative and prose poems. Exploration in the most classic and adventurous sense, contemporary urban life, the myths, tales, and customs of real and invented peoples, alternate as in a fugue in both books.

Roi des cent cavaliers (published in France by Flammarion in 2002) exists in the territory Étienne has created between poetry and prose, with all the poem's compression and making full use of its fertile paradoxes. It is a unified book consisting of nine sequences that enigmatically consider war, human relations, sex, nature, the contemporary world and its intersecting cultures, and the poet's own (international) history. Structurally, the book pivots on two numbers: fourteen, since each individual poem is a "prose (or prose-poem) sonnet," each of whose lines is a discrete sentence; and ten, along with its multiple, one hundred, as each sequence or "chapter" is composed of ten such sonnets, and the book as a whole, with its (numbered) titles and annotations included, comprises a hundred sections. The text is porous: there are collagings or interpolations of Marina Tsvetaeva, T. S. Eliot, Tristan Tzara, and others. Tsvetaeva's voice, or Étienne's re-creation of it, alternates with the narrator's in one sequence. Two of the most seemingly "surreal" sequences, each of which begins with the evocation of a painter and his surroundings, are, in fact, also descriptive "fugues" on themes in the work of two contemporary French graphic artists, Gaston Planet and François Dilasser. Who are the two protagonists, female and male, with vaguely Southeast Asian names, venturing through the jungles of fable, the architecture of dreams—or the airport in Atlanta, Georgia? Alternating with them is a first-person narrator whose "war diary" resembles most closely quotidian life in contemporary Paris, but whose experiences veer sharply away from the "possible" just when a reader begins to take her for the writer's avatar. Linking them all is "the child," an interlocutor, who passes in and out of all their stories. The book as a whole reflects, as in a mosaic of shattered mirrors, many of the writer's ongoing preoccupations: the potentially theatrical nature of writing on the page; the simultaneous construction/deconstruction of narrative; gender; the juxtaposition of Orient and Occident; an eroticism that is at once physical and cerebral; the extension of the limits of genre (poetry/prose/dramatic writing); an interpenetration of the quotidian and the foreign, in which the most "exotic" journeys become ordinary, and the most ordinary displacements partake of the disquieting and the strange.

—Marilyn Hacker
Paris, 2008

ROI DES
CENT CAVALIERS

KING OF A
HUNDRED HORSEMEN

1. La mer l'amour

1. Ocean / Emotion

2. Je pourrais raconter comment longtemps j'ai cru à la paralysie de ma mémoire : vingt ans passés hors de la France et que m'en restait-il ?

— Regarde bien, disait mon père, regarde bien, nous passons le canal de Suez !

J'avais sept ans, nous nous tenions debout sur le pont du bateau qui revenait de Cochinchine, l'eau en bas était loin, je me sentais perdue, perchée et minuscule.

J'ai oublié Suez, le canal important, je n'ai gardé que l'injonction, qui était de ne pas oublier, la sensation de ma hauteur au-dessus de la mer, l'inquiétude. Comment ne pas tomber ?

Je garde des images.

Contrairement à ma croyance, lorsque je vérifie elles sont toutes là.

Toutes, je ne sais pas, mais nombreuses, c'est certain, de plus en plus nombreuses au fur et à mesure que je tâte le sol de ma canne d'aveugle, le sol de ma maison secrète.

Je pourrais raconter que j'écrivis longtemps avec des lettres transparentes, comme celles des pâtes qui servent aux potages.

Et puis un jour, j'ai dit des mots avec ma voix, j'ai fait des gestes avec mon corps, nous jouions du théâtre, du moins nous apprenions, chaque partie de moi devenue clairvoyante.

J'inventais le réel :

Agathe à coeur de Cristobal.

Or la cristobalite est au coeur de l'agate.

2. I could tell you how for a long time I thought my memory was paralyzed: twenty years passed outside France and what have I left of it?

— Take a good look, said my father, take a good look, we're going through the Suez Canal!

I was seven years old, we were standing on the bridge of the boat that was returning from Cochin China, the water below was far away, I felt lost, perched like a bird, minuscule.

I have forgotten Suez, the significant canal, I've only kept the command, which was not to forget, the sensation of my height above the sea, the uneasiness. How not to fall?

I hold on to images.

Contrary to my belief, when I verify, they are all there.

All of them, I can't know that, but many, that's for sure, more and more of them as I tap the floor with my blind man's cane, the floor of my secret dwelling.

I could tell how for a long time I wrote with transparent letters, like the alphabet noodles they put in soups.

And then one day, I pronounced words with my voice, I made movements with my body, we were acting in the theater, at least we were learning to, each part of me became clairvoyant.

I invented the real:

Agatha with Cristobal's heart.

But then cristobalite is at the heart of agate.

Ou bien je retrouvais ce que j'avais peut-être, un jour ancien, appris.

J'écrivais Cappadoce, et je savais au même instant, moi qui ne savais rien, où était Cappadoce.

Au bord de la mer Noire.

Or I was rediscovering what I had perhaps, once, long ago, learned.

I would write Cappadocia, and I would know at the same instant, I who knew nothing, where Cappadocia was.

On the shore of the Black Sea.

3. Le puzzle existait, j'espérais peu à peu replacer ses morceaux. Éparpillés par quel effroi ?

Si on me demandait, tant d'années à écrire, est-ce bien raisonnable ? je pourrais essayer de répondre, expliquer.

J'ai le goût de la date et le sens de la dette, je suis là pour porter témoignage.

Notre quête cessera quand nous arriverons d'où nous étions partis, sachant le lieu pour la première fois.

À l'évidence écrire est un retour, un supplément à un voyage.

C'est pourquoi j'aimerais, pour l'occasion, m'appeler d'autres noms.

Ou prendre un autre sexe.

« Je suis un homme. »

C'est ce que dit Isé, je suis un homme, Isé qui rit, qui aime son mari comme on aime une femme.

Ce moment de ma vie, j'ai à peine eu le temps, je regardais ailleurs, il y avait, il y avait.

Le reconstituer ? Agendas, lettres, témoignages ? Ou le traquer ? Ou bien me perdre dans ses traces ?

Procéder autrement. Pour commencer biffer, m'intéresser à autre chose.

Je me dis rester calme, les mots dedans, les gens dehors, voilà mon flux. Encore plus calme. Surgit le moi sauvé, épars mais rassemblé.

Mémoire lacunaire ou mémoire absolue, je voyage à l'envers pour retrouver la mer.

3. The puzzle existed, I hoped gradually to put its pieces back in place. Scattered by what fright?

If anyone asked me, so many years spent writing, does that make any sense? I could try to answer, to explain.

I have a taste for dates and a sense of debt, I am there to bear witness.

Our quest will cease when we arrive at our point of departure, knowing the spot for the first time.

Obviously writing is a return, a supplement to a journey.

That's why I would like, on this occasion, to call myself by other names.

Or to assume another sex.

"I am a man."

That's what Isa used to say, I am a man, Isa who laughs, who loves her husband the way one loves a woman.

This moment of my life, I have hardly had time, I was looking elsewhere, there was, there was.

To put it back together? Date-books, letters, testimonies? Or to track it down? Or to lose myself in its tracks?

To proceed in a different way. To begin with, cross out lines, be interested in other things.

I say to myself, stay calm, words inside, people outside, there is my flow. Still calmer. The rescued word springs forth, scattered but gathered.

Lacunary memory or absolute memory, I travel backward to find the sea again.

4. « Il faut te dire, Boris, je n'aime pas la mer », écrivait Marina à Boris Pasternak.

Elle séjournait pourtant au bord de l'océan, à Saint-Gilles-sur-Vie.

Venue là de Paris, pour passer des vacances ?

Elle déjà exilée, que venait-elle chercher au sud de Noirmoutier ?

Dans ce bourg qui s'appelle à présent Saint-Gilles-Croix-de-Vie, « dénué de panache, buissons, sables et croix », elle court voir si la Vie remonte ou redescend.

La Vie est la rivière.

On dit parfois : la vie est un long fleuve.

Lorsqu'on est en Bretagne elle est plutôt la mer qui arrive et repart, qui dénude la terre, qui la transforme en sol de lune, puis qui revient, qui la recouvre.

Les yeux l'identifient quand elle a disparu, identifie le manque d'elle, à cause des presqu'îles et des îles bleutées qui marquent sa limite, ou le début du ciel.

La mer, dit Marina, elle est insurmontable et humiliante.

« . . . la dictature, Boris, et la fierté blessée. »

En attendant qu'elle revienne, ce qui semble jamais, la vase a pris la place, elle miroite comme l'eau.

Quelques rochers très noirs cassent sa platitude, on les croirait à contre-jour, on se croirait au crépuscule, près d'un cratère, d'une terre pétrifiée.

Cependant la lumière vient d'en haut, à travers une brume invisible.

4. "I must tell you, Boris, I don't like the sea," wrote Marina to Boris Pasternak.

She was nonetheless staying at the seashore, at Saint-Gilles-sur-Vie.

Come there from Paris, to spend her vacation?

Already in exile, what was she looking for south of Noirmoutier?

In that town which is now called Saint-Gilles-Croix-de-Vie "stripped of style, bushes, sand and crosses" she runs to see if la Vie flows upstream or downstream.

La Vie is the little river.

It's sometimes said: life is a long river.

When you're in Brittany, it's the sea, rather, that arrives and departs, that denudes the earth, transforms it into a moonscape, which then comes back, which recovers it.

Eyes notice when it has disappeared, identify its absence, because of the blue-tinged peninsulas and islands that mark its limit, or the beginning of the sky.

The sea, says Marina, is insurmountable and humiliating.

". . . dictatorship, Boris, and wounded pride."

While waiting for it to return, which it seems will be never, silt has replaced it, it glistens like water.

A few very black rocks break its flatness, you'd think the light was behind them, you'd think it was dusk, at the edge of a crater, near petrified earth.

Nevertheless, the light comes from above, through an invisible fog.

5. Sur la grève mouillée, des barques, des bateaux sont couchés sur le flanc, hors de leur élément.

« La terre a froid et je la plains, mais la mer n'a pas froid.

« C'est un plat monstrueux, un énorme berceau qui renverse l'enfant, je veux dire le navire.

« Je l'ai noté dans mon carnet pour te le dire, Boris. Je n'aime pas la mer, trop semblable à l'amour.

« Rester là à attendre. »

Je n'aime pas non plus les choses, raconte Marina, ceux qui entassent, qui vivent seuls, au milieu de leurs malles.

Étrange nuit que la nuit même.

Je n'aime que le diable, avec lui nous dansons sur les braises.

Ainsi font les Bretons avec leur diable à eux. Le vieux Pol, Vieux Guillaume, Petit Yves.

Quarquase de mort en bois, moulée ou peinte, Ankou.

Son pays est glacial et brumeux, il faut, pour y entrer, traverser un cours d'eau.

C'est le séjour des Anaons, les âmes mortes.

Lavandières de la nuit.

« La vie est une gare. Je partirai bientôt, pour où je ne sais pas. »

Chant et déchant. De Marina ou de la mer ?

5. On the wet shore, skiffs, boats, lying on their sides, out of their element.

"The earth is cold, and I am sorry for it, but the sea is not cold.

"It's a monstrous plate, a huge cradle that spills the child out, I mean the boat.

"I put that in my notebook to tell it to you, Boris. I don't like the sea, too much like love.

"To stay there, waiting."

I don't like things, either, writes Marina, or people who hoard them, who live alone, in the midst of their suitcases.

Strange night that night in itself.

I only like the devil, with him, we can dance on the embers.

That's what the Bretons do with their own devil. Old Paul, Old William, Little Yves.

Quarquase of the dead made of wood, molded or painted, Ankou.

His country is frozen and foggy, to enter it, one must cross a river.

It's the dwelling of the Anaons, the dead souls.

Laundresses of the night.

"Life is a train station. I will leave soon, for where I don't know."

Chant and disenchantment. Marina's or the sea's?

6. Le bus nous a conduits au port de La Pallice.

Paul est dehors sur le trottoir, j'attends dans un café.

Tout paraît pétrifié, les gens, le temps, le bus, enfin.

La mer est si boueuse qu'on dirait une terre, agitée sous l'écume.

Promenade en taxi à Saint-Martin-de-Ré, la Flotte-en-Ré, Marie-de-Ré.

La prison des bagnards, l'anse de pierre d'où les canaux partaient jusqu'au bateau-cellule.

Retour à la Rochelle.

Vols d'oiseaux, croix petites et noires.

Rue Sur-les-Murs, rue des Fagots, et rue des Trois-Moulins.

La tour de la Lanterne ou des Quatre-Sergents.

Nous habitons rue Sur-les-Murs, nous regardons la mer depuis notre maison, dès le matin jusqu'à la nuit.

Elle est boueuse ou elle est claire.

Je pense à la statue Moai kava kava, de l'île de Pâques. Elle a deux têtes, son bois est de Toromiro.

On ne voit que ses yeux d'obsidienne, cerclés d'un filet d'or.

6. The bus took us to the port at La Pallice.

Paul is outside, on the sidewalk, I wait in a café.

Everything seemed petrified, people, time, the bus, all that.

The sea is so muddy you'd say a field, stormy beneath the foam.

Trip in a taxi to Saint-Martin-de-Ré, la-Flotte-en-Ré, Marie-de-Ré.

The convicts' prison, the low stone arch from where the canals led up to the cell-boat.

Return to La Rochelle.

Birds in flight, little black crosses.

Rue Sur-les-Murs, rue des Fagots, and rue des Trois-Moulins.

The Lantern Tower, the Four Sergeants' Tower.

We live on rue Sur-les-Murs, we watch the sea from our house, from first thing in the morning till nightfall.

It's muddy or it's clear.

I think of the Moai kava kava statue on Easter Island. It has two heads, the wood it's carved of comes from Toromino.

One sees only its obsidian eyes, rimmed with a narrow gold line.

7. Les lunettes sont roses, les cheveux sont fendus au sommet de la tête et rassemblés en tresse unique, sur le côté.

Le cou est entouré par une écharpe jaune, qui fait le tour et qui descend.

La main gauche tient la tempe et le front, qui ne prétend pas aux pensées, ni à la pesanteur car la tempe et le front rient autant que la bouche, devant la porte peinte en bleu.

N'empêche.

Je suis personne déplacée dans un pays en guerre.

Je cherche la chanson, je dois la retrouver, la retrouver absolument, c'est une idée, c'est mon idée, ma seule idée.

La chanson est ancienne, à peine un souvenir qui insiste et qui brûle, qui ne s'attrape pas comme un plumet de foire, dans les manèges.

De temps en temps quand même je sors, de ma maison, de mon quartier et de ma ville.

Je sors, je bouge, on peut dire que je bouge, je suis bien avancée tout le long de ma vie, que je parcours en fredonnant la chanson très ancienne.

Je ne fredonne pas, je cherche la chanson perdue.

Retrouve-la, retrouve-la ! Je me fais du théâtre à moi-même, des discours, je m'exhorte, je me pousse au combat, je pousse aussi des cris sans gloire, aacchtt !

Quand je vivais en mer de Chine, je m'enfuyais avec Gérard, dans la mangrove, pour la chercher.

Je courais, je sautais, je me mettais la tête en bas, et regardais.

Entre les branches d'arbres le ciel n'existait pas, tout était inversé, difficile.

7. The glasses are pink, the hair parted at the top of the head and gathered in a single braid, down one side.

The neck is circled by a yellow scarf, which goes around and then down.

The left hand supports the temple and the forehead, which does not aspire to thoughts, nor to depth, for the temple and the forehead laugh as much as the mouth does, in front of the blue-painted door.

Nevertheless.

I am a displaced person in a country at war.

I'm seeking the song, I must find it, find it absolutely, it's an idea, it's my idea, my only idea.

The song is old, barely a memory that persists and burns, that cannot be grabbed like a feather at the fair, from the carousel.

From time to time I go out nevertheless, from my house, from my neighborhood, from my city.

I go out, I move, you could say I move, I'm quite advanced my whole life long, trajectory I pursue humming the very old song.

I'm not humming, I'm searching for the lost song.

Find it, find it! I perform for myself, speeches, I exhort myself, push myself into combat, also emit inglorious cries, arrgh!

When I lived on the China Sea, I would run off with Gerard into the mangrove swamp, to look for it.

I ran, I jumped, I put my head down between my legs and looked.

Between the trees' branches, there was no more sky, everything was upside down, difficult.

8. En remontant la mer d'Oman, je la cherchais sur le navire qui fendait l'eau, avec la conviction de sa grandeur.

Il était pourtant vieux, éprouvé.

Il crachait du charbon et donnait de la bonde sur un bord, le vent était trop fort, sa cargaison mal répartie.

Sur la lagune d'Ebrié, je la cherchais à bicyclette en dévalant la côte qui menait à l'école où monsieur Parisot enseignait les histoires de l'histoire et les chiffres des tables et les lettres des fables et les conjugaisons.

Ah les conjugaisons !

Quand j'habitais le Suñugal, je la cherchais dans la poussière qui montait des chemins, qui recouvrait les pieds des hommes et les palais d'argile.

Fatigue séculaire, comme inventée, semblable me disais-je, à la musique très perdue.

Quand je revins à l'Ile-en-France, l'hiver était fréquent, l'hiver me surprenait.

Je connaissais l'été, rien que l'été, j'éprouvais que j'avais traversé la frontière dans le sens du retour, de la fin de l'exil.

Tant d'années, me disais-je, d'un côté, tant d'années d'un côté et maintenant de l'autre sans que j'y aie pris garde ?

C'était à n'y pas croire, c'était à croire que ma tête !

La lumière filtrait à travers mes paupières d'endormi ou d'oiseau, qu'un maître dur avait cousues.

À présent me disais-je, tout sera différent, familier.

La chanson très ancienne habite quelque part, dans le pays aimé. N'est-il pas vrai ?

8. Sailing back up the sea of Oman, I searched for it on the steamer cleaving the water, convinced of its grandeur.

And yet the boat was old, well worn.

It spit coal and listed to one side, the wind was too strong, the cargo badly distributed.

On Ebrié Lagoon, I looked for it on my bicycle racing along the coast that led to school where Monsieur Parisot taught the stories of history and the numbers of tables and the letters of fables and conjugations.

Oh, conjugations!

When I lived in Suñugal, I looked for it in the dust that came up the roads, that covered people's feet and clay palaces.

Secular fatigue, something invented, similar, I told myself, to very lost music.

When I came back to Île-de-France, winter was frequent, winter surprised me.

I knew summer, nothing but summer, I felt that I had crossed the frontier in the direction of a return, of exile's end.

So many years, I said to myself, on one side, so many years on one side and now on the other without my noticing?

It was not to be believed, my eye, it was to be believed (was I going crazy?).

Light filtered through my lids, a sleeping woman's or a bird's, sewn shut by a harsh master.

Now, I said to myself, everything will be different, familiar.

The very old song lives somewhere, in the beloved country. Isn't that true?

9. Dans mon enfance, j'avais appris à courir vite autour des tables.

Plus je courais, moins je me faisais prendre.

Les Père Noël exacts venaient jusqu'aux tropiques, ils m'apportaient des livres, que je lisais, réécrivais.

Je les ouvrais avec mes doigts en les tenant par le milieu, pas besoin d'outillage.

On m'appelait cher douloureux.

J'avais appris très tôt ce qu'il en coûte de porter. Mes fardeaux, par la suite ne firent qu'augmenter.

C'était la guerre, je n'en revenais pas, je ne m'en remis pas.

Nous étions partis loin, je m'habituais à être ailleurs, le non nommé.

J'insiste donc : écrire, c'est prendre son élan pour démêler le blanc.

Les Barbares étaient deux, étaient dix, étaient mille, on ne les voyait pas mais on les entendait.

Petites rues à angles droits. Derrière les volets clos, les ombres d'une fête.

Quand j'arrivai dans le jardin, les invités tournaient les broches, les femmes s'asseyaient au milieu de leur robe.

Chacun mangeait à pleines mains le riz et le poisson dans des cuvettes émaillées.

Velours, suint des agneaux.

9. In my childhood, I had learned how to run quickly around tables.

The more I ran, the less often I was caught.

Punctual Santa Clauses came all the way to the tropics, they brought me books that I would read, rewrite.

I cut the pages with my fingers holding them down the middle, no need of any tools.

They called me dear sorrowful one.

I had learned very early what it cost to carry that. My burdens, afterwards, only grew.

It was wartime, I didn't get away from that, I didn't get over that.

We had gone far away, I got used to being elsewhere, the unnamed.

So I insist: to write is to take a running start on untangling the blanks.

There were two Barbarians, were ten, were a thousand, you couldn't see them but you heard them.

Little right-angled streets. Behind closed shutters, the shadows of a party.

When I arrived in the garden, guests were turning the spits, women seated in the midst of their dresses.

Everyone was eating handfuls of rice and fish from enameled bowls.

Velvet, lamb suint.

10. On m'avait épousée, donné le pain, blancheur du voile, cire du cierge.

On m'avait regardée, comme un oiseau j'étais montée.

La mer hors des limites, elle dépassait l'entendement, trop grosse, la dune commencée, recommencée sous le ciel ferme.

Dans l'espace du vent les coquillages respiraient.

La guerre dura longtemps. Quand on sortait on ne revenait pas ou maquillé de sang.

La femme du banquier battait le beurre dans le jardin, les doigts bagués.

J'entendais vivre au moins pour voir. Je ne vis pas grand-chose.

Car il y a l'ordre moral, et en dessous, inextricables, les grandes tables de la loi.

Le destin même y perd la force.

Je me prenais pour un insecte, je regardais les gens de biais, pour ainsi dire par le côté.

Il m'arrivait aussi, pensez donc quelle audace, de me sentir confuse de ma suprématie.

— Les animaux sont sages, ils sont des saints, disait l'enfant.

— Des fois je pense que je voudrais ne pas penser, lui répondait la vieille dame.

Dans la maison notoirement instable, l'enfant chantait la ballade du soldat.

10. I had been married, given the bread, whiteness of the veil, the candle's wax.

I had been looked at, like a bird I was mounted.

The sea spilling its limits, it was beyond comprehension, too full, the dune begun, begun again beneath the solid sky.

In the wind's space the seashells breathed.

The war lasted a long time. When someone went out, they didn't come back, or came back rouged with blood.

The banker's wife churned butter in the garden, rings on her fingers.

I intended to live at least to see. I did not see much.

For there's the moral order, and below it, inextricable, the great tablets of the law.

Even fate loses its force there.

I took myself for an insect, I looked at people indirectly, as it were, from the side.

It happened also (think of the audacity) that I'd feel embarrassed about my superiority.

— Animals are wise, they are saints, said the child.

— Sometimes I think that I'd like not to think, the old lady answered him.

In the notoriously unstable house, the child sang the ballad of the soldier.

11. J'ai voyagé ma vie durant dans des pays aux noms superbes. Je suis entré dans leurs légendes comme si j'étais moi-même un roi.

« But I'm also keen on roses. »

J'ai remonté les fleuves jaunes dans des bateaux rapetassés, escaladé les mille monts et traversé les marécages.

« But I'm also keen on roses. »

Dans ces pays devenus miens j'ai construit routes et maisons, ponts, aqueducs et voies ferrées, nourri, soigné parfois guéri.

« But I'm also keen on roses. »

J'y ai aussi porté le feu de nos canons et de nos bombes, détruit, tué, enseveli car ces pays n'étaient pas miens.

« But I'm also keen on roses. »

Mais à présent je me repose entre la mer et la montagne, je lis les livres pour comprendre quel est le sens de toute chose.

« But I'm also keen on roses. »

11. I've traveled my whole life long in countries with splendid names. I've entered into their legends as if I were a king myself.

"Pero me gustan también las rosas."

I've made my way up yellow rivers in patched-up boats, climbed the thousand peaks and crossed the marshlands.

"Pero me gustan también las rosas."

In those countries become my own, I have built roads and houses, bridges, aqueducts and railroads, fed, cared for and sometimes healed.

"Pero me gustan también las rosas."

I have also brought the fire of our cannons and our bombs, destroyed, killed, buried, for these countries were not my own.

"Pero me gustan también las rosas."

But at present I live at ease between the sea and the mountains, I read books to understand the meaning of each thing.

"Pero me gustan también las rosas."

12. La preuve par les oiseaux

12. Proof by the Birds

13. Personne ne voit personne.

De temps en temps, quelqu'un va jusqu'au fond, on ne s'en remet pas, il a touché, mais quoi ?

On reste ouvert à lui.

L'enfant était dehors, devant le ciel : — La nuit est toujours bleue.

Elle rêvait qu'elle perdait ses chaussures, perdait ses vêtements.

Le jardin, la maison étaient très éclairés, les femmes belles.

La maîtresse de maison, qui s'était absentée, voulait rentrer chez elle.

Des policiers barraient l'entrée : — Prouvez-nous qui vous êtes.

Elle répondait : — Je m'appelle Ang.

— Le docteur du quartier ne vous a jamais vue, lui répliquait un policier.

L'obscurité, le vent.

Quelqu'un, dans la maison, se lamentait.

— Vous l'avez arraché, il était encore bon, il aurait pu fleurir.

Quelqu'un prenait de la distance, pour vomir une pâte ondulée, consistante.

13. No one sees anyone.

From time to time, someone goes all the way to the bottom, no one can get over it, he touched something, but what?

One stays open to him.

The child was outside, facing the sky: — The night is always blue.

She dreamed that she lost her shoes, lost her clothes.

The garden, the house, were brightly lit, the women beautiful.

The mistress of the house, who had gone out, wanted to return home.

Policemen barred the doorway: — Prove to us who you are!

She answered: — My name is Ang.

— The local doctor has never seen you, a policeman answered her.

Darkness, wind.

Someone, in the house, was wailing.

— You've uprooted it, it was still good, it might have flowered.

Someone moved away, to vomit up a wavy, consistent dough.

14. On reconnaissait Ang, qui cherchait à extraire des matières de sa bouche.

Des herbes ou de la chair qui n'étaient pas son corps, qui occupaient son corps sans obstruer sa gorge.

Comme elle tirait, il en venait un peu mais pas suffisamment.

Tirait encore, c'était un vrai travail, sans espoir, agaçant.

Le menton et les joues maculés, elle essayait de s'essuyer, mais manquait de mouchoir.

Un policier tendait le sien.

Elle refusait, méfiante, le sentant versatile, prêt à l'hostilité, ou désireux de se distraire, s'amuser d'elle.

Je ne me plaindrai pas, se disait-elle en parcourant la rue très large, à travers son quartier.

Tout ce qui, dans sa vie, avait une importance, était situé là.

La rue n'était pas goudronnée, la rue était un fleuve, son cours était doré, terrestre et non liquide.

Sur ses rives deux murs bas servaient à séparer son sable des trottoirs.

Tout au bout, une place, en terre comme la rue, et comme elle soulevée d'un vent fort.

— Où est le responsable ? demandait Ang aux secrétaires qui travaillaient à leur fenêtre.

— En tournée d'inspection, répondaient-elles.

14. One could recognize Ang, who was trying to extract things from her mouth.

Weeds or flesh that were not her body, which occupied her body without blocking her throat.

As she pulled, some of it came out, but not enough.

Pulled again, it was a real effort, hopeless, annoying.

Her chin and her cheeks stained, she tried to wipe herself off, but she had no handkerchief.

A policeman offered his.

She refused, wary, sensing he was fickle, ready to turn hostile, or wanting to distract himself, to mock her.

I won't complain, she thought, crossing the very wide street, through her neighborhood.

Everything that, in her life, had any importance was located there.

The street was not tarred, the street was a river, its course was golden, earthly and not liquid.

On its banks two low walls served to separate its sand from the sidewalks.

Right at the end, a square, earthen like the street, and like the street stirred up by a strong wind.

— Where is the person in charge? Ang asked the secretaries who were working near their window.

— On a tour of inspection, they answered.

15. Elle dépassa l'église à gauche, elle traversa la place et parvint à la poste.

On dirait une école, la mairie d'un village, pensa Ang.

Elle entra.

Sur le panneau de bois à droite, des papiers punaisés.

C'était de fins feuillets recouverts de sa propre écriture, qu'elle avaient envoyés et qui lui revenaient.

Mais l'enveloppe était ouverte et les feuillets sortaient, comme les choses de son gosier.

À côté des feuillets, sur le panneau de bois, un message, griffonné.

Le Rayonnant part en voyage.

C'est ainsi qu'elle nommait son mari.

Il reprenait le mot, il la frappait avec le mot.

Elle recevait le coup, sortait, pliée, sur le trottoir, où l'attendait l'enfant.

Plus tard, quand elle se coucherait, elle serait un feuillet qui a froid.

L'enfant dirait :

— Il fait trop beau pour s'endormir.

15. She passed the church on the left, she crossed the square and reached the post office.

It looks like a school, like a village town hall, Ang thought.

She entered.

On the wooden panel to her right, papers tacked up.

They were fine sheets covered with her own handwriting, which she had sent, and which came back to her.

But the envelope was open, and the sheets came out, like the things from her gullet.

Beside the sheets of paper, on the wooden panel, a message, scribbled.

The Radiant One is leaving on a journey.

That was what she used to call her husband.

He took the word back, he struck her with the word.

She received the blow, went out, bent over, on the sidewalk where the child was waiting for her.

Later, when she went to bed, she would be a sheet of paper that was cold.

The child said:

— It's too beautiful out to go to sleep.

16. La délectable certitude.

Elle rencontrait l'Amer, souriant et vif, qui l'invitait à un voyage.

— Nous partirons.

Ils partirent en effet.

Le parc au pied de la fenêtre, ses arbres centenaires.

Un songe proche.

On ne pouvait s'y promener, on ne pouvait que regarder.

Une promesse. Toute promesse.

L'Amer disait :

— Tu es la seule. Et puis : — Faisons l'amour encore.

Elle répondait : — Oui mais souvent. Et lui, inquiet : — C'était donc bien ?

Il l'embrassait, elle inquiète à son tour : — Non pas devant les autres.

— Si, justement.

Une vendeuse de fleurs passait, les séparait, désespérante. Ang la chassait, la vendeuse menaçait, fleurs aux poings : — Tu ressembles à la mort.

16. The delectable certainty.

She met the Bitter One, smiling and lively, who invited her on a trip.

— We'll go away.

And they did go away.

The park at the foot of the window, its hundred-year-old trees.

A nearby dream.

Impossible to walk there, one could only look.

A promise. Entirely a promise.

The Bitter One said:

— You are the only one. And then: — Let's make love again.

She answered: — Yes, but often. And he, uneasily: — Was it good, then?

He kissed her, she in her turn uneasy: — Not in front of the others.

— Yes, that's just what I meant.

A flower-vendor passed, hopeless, separated them. Ang chased her away, the vendor threatened her, fists full of flowers: — You look like death.

17. Conversation. Excitation.

Et surenchère.

On crie. Fatigue.

La campagne, au-dehors, magnifique.

On gouverne très peu. Mais au moins décider du possible.

Toute idée de la mort ramène au désamour. Toute mort : celle-là.

L'effort pour être au monde. La lutte.

Garder les yeux ouverts quand les paupières pèsent.

Un cauchemar.

L'éveil et le salut.

Iniquité de la conversation.

Merveille de l'écrit, goût de l'écrit.

Ce sont les autres qui épuisent.

Ma quantité de solitude nécessaire.

17. Conversation. Excitement.

And overblown promises.

One cries out. Fatigue.

The countryside, outdoors, magnificent.

One governs minimally. But at least decides what's possible.

Every idea of death leads back to the lack of love. Every death: to that one.

The effort to be in the world. The struggle.

To keep one's eyes open when one's eyelids are weighed down.

A nightmare.

Awakening and salvation.

The injustice of conversation.

Marvel of writing, taste for writing.

It's others who are exhausting.

My necessary dose of solitude.

18. Faire ailleurs autre chose.

Ne pas voir, pas savoir.

Épuiser sa fatigue. S'en défaire. Se refaire ?

À défaut de comprendre, prendre ce qui n'est pas, aller où lui n'est pas.

C'est le soir, en l'absence du soleil, que l'angoisse la prend.

Entre la peur du bout et celle de maintenant, la hâte extrême du présent, se succèdent les peurs, celle des morts possibles.

Et, redoutée, surtout : celle qu'il inflige quand il s'en va.

C'est immédiatement. On se dépêche. C'est maintenant.

— Je veux t'emplir.

— Mais tu m'emplis. Quand tu t'éloignes je te perds.

Il secouait la tête, sceptique.

Il est froid.

Il retient et il chasse.

Beaucoup plus doux et attentif et désireux de ne point nuire qu'il n'y paraît d'abord.

Muet quant aux mots maîtres. Sa passion veut le corps.

18. To do something else elsewhere.

Not to see, not to know.

To exhaust one's fatigue. Divest oneself of it. Reinvent oneself?

For lack of taking it in, to take what it isn't, to go where he is not.

It's in the evening, in the sun's absence, when anguish seizes her.

Between fear of the end and fear of the moment, the terrible swiftness of the present, fears follow on each other, the fear of possible deaths.

And, especially dreaded, the one he inflicts when he leaves.

It's right away. They hurry. It's now.

— I want to fill you up.

— But you do fill me. When you move away from me, I lose you.

He shook his head, skeptical.

He is cold.

He holds back and he chases away.

Much gentler and attentive and desirous of doing no harm than it first seemed.

Mute for the key words. His passion wants the body.

19. L'amour se règle-t-il, Seigneur, sur l'injustice ? Assassinant qui le chérit, par pur caprice.

La vie finit bientôt.

Ils partaient vers les bois.

Ang se voyait couchée, tranquille, parmi les herbes pour dormir.

Près de la route, on allongeait une infirmière, on la couvrait d'un drap.

La fée des bois s'en approchait pour la couper en tranches avec de grands ciseaux.

Sur le chemin, Ang le savait, il y aurait la mort, un grand cadavre dévoré.

La nuit dernière aussi, il y avait la mort.

— Je dois aller au cimetière de mon village, disait l'enfant, on m'y enterrera plus tard.

— Moi je veux qu'on me mette dans la terre du manège, sous les pieds des chevaux, répondait son amie qui était cavalière.

Sur le chemin Ang serait seule.

Elle se souvient quand il disait :

— Rappelle-toi le rôle, ce sera le dernier et on t'y verra vieille. Il parlait à l'actrice.

Quand même, s'étonnait Ang, la maison m'appartient, elle s'agrandit quand je l'explore, poussant les murs sans cesse.

19. Does love, O Lord, model itself on injustice? Murdering the one who cherishes it, by pure caprice.

Life is soon over.

They were heading for the woods.

Ang saw herself stretched out in the grass, calmly, to sleep.

Near the road, they were laying a nurse down, covering her with a sheet.

The fairy of the woods approached to slice her in pieces with a pair of shears.

On the road, Ang knew it, death would be there, a huge devoured corpse.

The previous night also, there had been death.

— I must go to the cemetery in my village, said the child, they will bury me there later.

— Me, I'd like to be buried under the dressage ring, beneath the horses' feet, replied his friend, already a horsewoman.

On the road, Ang would be alone.

She recalls him saying:

— Remember your role, it will be the last one, and you'll be old in it. He was talking to the actress.

All the same, Ang marveled, the house belongs to me, it expands when I explore it, constantly pushing the wall.

20. — Je veux n'aimer que toi, je ne veux pas te perdre.
Tu es lyrique.

Ses yeux. Décrire un jour ses yeux.

Et sa légèreté, ses membres fins.

Ang veut le regarder, le regarder, le regarder.

Son terrible visage.

La passion froide. La passion sèche comme un bois.

Pour toi mon corps est nu, et ses parties fragiles, plus
nues d'être fragiles, plus fragiles d'être nues.

— C'est sûrement trop tard, dit-il.

Quand on meurt très très fort, est-ce qu'on meurt ?

— Dis-moi ce que tu veux, dit-il, mais violemment.

Il n'a pas de cuirasse, il n'a pas de croyance, son sexe est
au milieu.

Il était là dans la maison où elle dormait, elle le voyait,
elle se levait, elle l'embrassait les yeux fermés.

Il l'embrassait heureux.

« Toute preuve par les oiseaux est étrange. »

20. — I want to love no one but you, I don't want to lose you. You are lyrical.

His eyes. To describe his eyes one day.

And his lightness, his slender limbs.

Ang wants to look at him, to look at him, to look at him.

His unbearable face.

Cold passion. Passion as dry as a stick.

For you my body is naked, and its fragile parts, more naked for being fragile, more fragile for being naked.

— It's surely too late, he says.

When you die hard, very hard, do you die?

— Tell me what you want, he says, but violently.

He has no breastplate, he has no beliefs, his sex is at the center.

He was there in the house where she slept, she saw him, she got up, kissed him with her eyes closed.

He kissed her, happy.

"Any proof by the birds is strange."

21. À la table voisine, un homme mange, un autre arrive.

Celui qui mange dit :

— Installe-toi.

Cependant son visage est fermé, on peut se demander s'il ne contredit pas l'invitation à s'installer.

L'autre hésite, fait même mine de partir, se ravise et s'assied.

À titre exceptionnel, pour se réconforter, il va manger tous les desserts.

C'est un homme à ne rien partager. Il me plaît, pense Ang.

Vers le fond du café, une femme s'agite.

Le garçon crie :

— J'appelle la police.

Elle sort son passeport :

— Je viens de loin, excusez-moi. Laissez-moi m'en aller, demain je reviendrai.

Mais le garçon est intraitable.

Dois-je payer pour elle ? Ang ne sait pas.

21. At the next table, a man is eating, another one arrives.

The one who is eating says:

— Have a seat.

But his face is closed tight, one might ask oneself if it doesn't contradict the invitation to join him.

The second man hesitates, makes as if to leave, changes his mind and sits down.

In this exceptional circumstance, to make himself feel better, he will eat all the desserts.

That's a man who doesn't share anything. I like him, thinks Ang.

Toward the rear of the café, a woman makes a fuss.

The waiter shouts:

— I'm going to call the police.

She takes out her passport:

— I come from far away, forgive me. Let me go, I'll come back tomorrow.

But the waiter is adamant.

Should I pay for her? Ang doesn't know.

22. Un cauchemar. Ang l'acceptait, un fois encore.

Un cauchemar. Elle cherchait à le voir, en vain, pour dire adieu.

L'aliénation par le bienfait. Obéis-moi car je te crée.

Tout homme est un danger.

C'est l'amour même qui la menace.

Elle a besoin, pour exister, d'être sous garantie.

Je dois vivre sans lui, je dois sortir de sa lumière.

Eh bien, je sors de sa lumière.

Quelques principes, seulement quelques-uns.

Le monde est modelable, ça se sculpte le monde et en soi quelle force !

Malgré tout le plaisir car le ravage en fin de compte, comme une drogue.

Se calmer, pour savoir le savoir.

Calme calme l'amour.

Que cesse la torsion du sens, la honte de l'amour, pour penser la pensée.

22. A nightmare. Ang accepted it, once more.

A nightmare. She was trying to see him, in vain, to say farewell.

Alienation by kindness. Obey me because I create you.

Every man is a danger.

It's love itself that threatens her.

In order to exist, she needs to be guaranteed.

I've got to live without him, I must get out of his light.

Well then, I get out of his light.

A few principles, only a few.

The world is malleable, the world can be sculpted and such force in oneself!

Pleasure in spite of everything since devastation is at the end of it, like a drug.

To calm oneself down, to know knowledge.

Calm love calm.

Let the contortion of the senses cease, the shame of love, so one can think one's thoughts.

23. Journal de guerre

23. War Diary

24. *Le 6 mai.* Je n'aime que la rue qui ressemble à la mer, le macadam et les pavés, dans la lumière du bus.

Il y a des flambées, des retombées, sommeil.

J'ai tant souffert depuis l'été.

Et à présent, sommeil.

Ne pas me réveiller. Je regarde Paris.

Le plaisir de la ville, de celle-là précisément.

C'est le printemps.

Je suis seule dans le bus, à l'arrière et debout.

La tentation de la réminiscence. La tradition des larmes.

On croit que la douleur, toute douleur.

On croit que le désir, que le plaisir, que l'émerveillement.

On croit que tout peut arriver.

On croit au seul qui croît en soi.

C'etait l'erreur qu'il faut commettre.

24. May 6. I only love the street that looks like the sea, the macadam and the pavement, in the bus lights.

There are flare-ups, fallout, sleep.

I've suffered so much, since summer.

And at present, sleep.

Not to wake up. I look at Paris.

The pleasure of the city, of this one precisely.

It's spring.

I'm alone on the bus, at the back, standing up.

The temptation of reminiscence. The tradition of tears.

One believes that grief, all grief.

One believes that desire, that pleasure, that wonder.

One believes that anything can happen.

One believes in the only one growing within.

It was the necessary error.

25. *Sans date.* Section des sexes.

Les mêmes mots mais les mots mêmes sont (un blanc).

Ce serait donc la guerre ?

Je me sens innocente.

La guerre des sexes. Il se méfie de tous.

Je me sens paresseuse.

J'ai rêvé de section car moi aussi peut-être.

Je croyais autrefois que castrer consistait à couper le phallus.

Je rêvais qu'une soeur avait par moi le vît coupé.

Dans mon rêve je tenais le morceau qui restait d'une main.

Et de l'autre, le morceau sectionné.

Tous deux bandaient et je songeais :

Rassemblés quelle taille.

Rassemblés quelle vie !

25. Undated. Sectioning of sexes.

The same words but the words themselves are (a blank).

Would it be war then?

I feel that I'm innocent.

The war between the sexes. He distrusts everyone.

I feel that I'm lazy.

I dreamed of amputation because I too perhaps.

I used to believe that castration meant cutting off the phallus.

I was dreaming that a sister had her member cut off by me.

In my dream I held the remaining part in one hand.

And in the other the amputated part.

Each part had an erection and I was musing:

Put together what a size!

Put together what a life!

26. Le 6 juin. Qu'étions-nous d'être nous ?

Amants, amants, soumis naguère à nos partages !

Peut-être n'y a-t-il qu'à s'enfermer dans le soleil ?

Un passant dans la gare :

— T'énerve pas c'est un tango.

Maladie, consentir, pendant un temps se reposer.

La maison est instable, mais on s'en accommode.

Comme du reste.

Tandis que lui, penché vers moi et par-dessus la table :

— Tu es si pure, je me sens très coupable.

Si beau, penché, coupable, et elle, la pure qui se demande :

— Qu'est-ce qu'il raconte ?

Essayant de remettre à l'endroit son visage, elle tient ses mains dedans.

26. June 6. What have we been to have become ourselves?

Lovers, lovers, long ago subject to what we shared!

Perhaps it's enough to lock ourselves up in the sun?

A passerby in the train station:

— Don't make a fuss, it's a tango.

Illness, to consent, to rest for a while.

The house is unstable, but one gets accustomed to it.

To it all.

While he, leaning toward me and over the table:

— You are so pure, I feel very guilty.

So handsome, leaning, guilty, and she, the pure one who asks herself:

— What's he going on about?

Trying to put her face back in place, she keeps her hands inside.

27. Été. La reconstitution qui suit peut au besoin se dispenser de justifications.

La montagne a un nom, c'est l'envers de l'endroit, ou revers, ou Revest.

Pourtant elle monte droit.

Dans le hameau, la vie était tranquille, quelquefois difficile.

On s'en accommodait, on vivait à son aise et cela suffisait.

La falaise servait à supprimer les animaux malades.

On les mettait au bord, on les poussait. Les corbeaux arrivait.

Aux fêtes de Saint-Jean, les pénitents se saluaient avec la croix qu'ils portaient haut, devant la procession.

À la gare un gros homme criait :

— T'as encore oublié ton pépin ?

Ang rêvait de la Chine.

N'en voyait que le rose qui doublait ses paupières.

Le gros homme répétait :

— T'as encore oublié ton pépin ?

27. *Summer.* The reconstitution that follows can, if need be, do without justification.

The mountain has a name, it's the back of the place, or reverse, or Revest.

And yet it goes straight up.

In the hamlet, life was peaceful, sometimes stressful.

One got used to it, one lived comfortably and that was enough.

The cliff was used to dispose of sick animals.

They were placed at the edge, they were pushed off. The crows arrived.

On Midsummer's Eve, the penitents greeted each other with the cross they were holding aloft at the head of the procession.

In the train station a fat man cried out:

— Forgotten your brolly again?

Ang dreamed of China.

Saw nothing of it but the pink that lined her eyelids.

The fat man repeated:

— Forgotten your brolly again?

28. *16 septembre.*

Nomenclature une.

« Elle naquit au bord du Tage où parfois la cavale tourne au vent sa mâchoire. »

Nomenclature deux.

Énumérer des personnages, leur donner quelque chose.

Une pensée heureuse, la mémoire d'un faux pas.

La couleur d'une robe, le regret d'être là ou de ne pas y être.

Le plaisir de marcher, le plaisir de marcher, le plaisir de marcher.

Le rétrécissement, le va-et-vient et l'inconfort.

L'inconfort de la lutte, l'espace indéchiffrable, l'espèce d'abattement qui peut saisir parfois.

Il avait dit :

— Je n'avais jamais rien connu de semblable depuis.

Comme si c'était la première fois.

Cette fois-là.

28. September 16.
First taxonomy.
"She was born on the banks of the Tage where sometimes the filly turns her muzzle into the wind."
Second taxonomy.
To list the characters, to give them something.

A happy thought, the memory of an error.

The color of a dress, regret at either being there or not.

The pleasure of walking, the pleasure of walking, the pleasure of walking.

The shrinkage, the coming and going and the discomfort.

The discomfort of the struggle, the indecipherable space, the kind of dejection that can sometimes come over one.

He had said:

— I had never known anything like it since then.

As if it were the first time.

That time.

29. 18 septembre.

Nomenclature trois.

Il y a une femme qui m'envoie un poème en flamand. Une autre en bas, qui boite et qui sourit.

Il y a des statues, dehors sur l'esplanade. Dedans, abandonnées, qui servent de jalons.

Il y a des armures dans des malles, marquées au nom de Jean Vilar.

Des costumes qu'on repasse, qu'on suspend à des cintres.

Des décors qu'on démonte et qu'on coupe à la hache.

Des glaces sans reflet.

Il y a des acteurs. Des entrées, des sorties.

Des saluts et des chats.

Il y a un baiser, deux baisers, trois baisers.

Il n'y a plus personne à qui penser dans le bonheur.

Les femmes sur les fresques ont besoin de la nuit pour ne pas s'effacer.

Continuer à porter l'édifice.

29. September 18
Third taxonomy.
There is a woman who sends me a poem in Flemish.
Another one downstairs, limping and smiling.

There are statues, outdoors on the esplanade.

Indoors, abandoned, that serve as milestones.

There is armor in trunks, marked with the name of
Jean Vilar.

Costumes that one irons, hangs up on hangers.

Scenery one dismantles and hacks up with an axe.

Mirrors without reflections.

There are actors. Entrances, exits.

Curtain-calls and cats.

There is a kiss, two kisses, three kisses.

There is no longer anyone to think of in times of joy.

The women in the frescoes need night in order not to
fade away.

To go on holding up the building.

30. Janvier. On n'écrit plus de poésie, un bric-à-brac de vieux droguiste.

Quel crédit accorder aux mots qui se succèdent, comment les croire encore possibles ?

Luttant contre le rythme pair, on ne tient plus sa main portée contre son coeur : le genre noble a la nausée.

On balade ses mots, on les décroche, on les espace, on les efface.

On les dispose comme on peint, comme on dessine ou comme on brode, au point de croix.

On fait de petits tas, sans ponctuation, « mendiant presque d'écrire ».

Des gens se parlent, parlent.

Dehors paraît, mais la chronologie, la logique sont absentes.

Restent des flaques.

« Ce n'est pas un poème en ce mois de janvier. »

Ce n'est pas un roman qui déroule une histoire, pourtant là, travestie par les larmes, l'incohérence du sourire.

Les dialogues s'estompent, ils sont de la pensée répétée en écho.

On évoque un silence, des doigts sur une vitre, une démarche entre des tables.

Comme on est bienveillant, on dit le chant et la lumière.

30. January. No one writes poetry any longer, bric-a-brac in an old hardware store.

What credence can be granted to words following each other, how can they still be thought possible?

Struggling against the even rhythm, one no longer holds one's hand to one's heart: the high old style till you're sick of it.

One walks one's words, one detaches them, spaces them, erases them.

One places them like a painter, as one would draw or embroider, cross-stitch.

One makes little piles, with no punctuation, "almost begging to write."

People talk to each other, talk.

The outside appears, but chronology, logic, are lacking. Puddles remain.

"This is not a poem in this month of January."

This is not a novel unrolling its story, yet there, disguised by tears, a smile's incoherence.

Dialogues fade out, they are made of thought, repeated by an echo.

A silence is invoked, fingers on a windowpane, a step taken between tables.

Since one is benevolent, one says song and light.

31. Tout cela apparaît à travers une brume invisible.

On se tient dans la neige du voyage, dans sa propre faiblesse, « sa très subtile force ».

Dans un sommeil intense et vif, une émotion qui paralyse, une servilité.

On a cessé d'être une, inviolable. Dans quel état se trouve-t-on ?

« Le mot de sodomie lui parvint à l'esprit. »

Car la neige bloque tout.

On se sent encagée, ramenée à un rêve vécu.

On vit des noces avec un homme épais.

Il est puissant ou feint de l'être. Il donne des conseils.

Debout ou accroupie on connaît la descente aux enfers.

On s'accomplit comme on se tue, on se dévêt comme on se jette, détruisant ce qu'on aime en l'aimant.

On s'abandonne. Ainsi dit-on. On s'abandonne dans l'amour. Ou plutôt le désir.

Puissance incontrôlée, cataclysme possible.

Devant n'importe qui, n'importe quoi, on garde l'impression d'être dévisagée dans la surprise.

31. All this appears through an invisible mist.

One persists through the snow of the journey, in one's own weakness, "its very subtle strength."

In an intense and lively sleep, an emotion that paralyzes, a servility.

One has ceased to be singular, inviolable. In what state does one find oneself?

"The word sodomy came to his mind."

Because the snow blocks everything.

One feels caged, brought back to a lived-through dream.

One goes through a wedding to a thick man.

He is powerful or pretends to be. He gives advice.

Standing up or squatting one knows the descent into hell.

One is fulfilled as one would kill oneself, strips as one would leap, destroying what is loved in loving it.

One abandons oneself. That's the expression. To abandon oneself in love. Or rather in desire.

Uncontrolled potency, possible cataclysm.

Before no matter whom, no matter what, the feeling remains of being stared at in surprise.

32. Mars. On est chez le coiffeur, cheveux mouillés, tête petite.

Les autres sont déjà casquées, assises.

Un jeune homme est debout, il s'affaire.

On garde son carnet et son stylo ouverts.

— Vous notez vos mémoires ?

Écrire est ridicule. Si on écrit on fait ses comptes, ceux du marché, du mois.

Mais pas ceux de sa vie.

On continue quand même à aligner ses chiffres, c'est-à-dire ses lettres.

On paraît moins vivant, on s'enfonce loin d'eux, qui sont dehors, à la surface, qui tiennent le bon bout de cette suite d'actes.

On extrait des fragments d'une suite, au hasard.

En vérité pas au hasard.

On les dispose, on les essaie, on les attache.

Jusqu'à ce qu'à son tour on tienne le bon bout.

Jusqu'à ce qu'à leur tour ils tiennent bien ensemble.

32. *March.* One is at the hairdresser's, hair wet, head small.

The others are already under the dryers, seated.

A young man is standing, he's bustling about.

One's kept a notebook and a pen open.

— You're writing your memoirs?

Writing is ridiculous. Whoever writes keeps accounts, of the market, of the month.

But not of a life.

One continues nonetheless to line up figures, that is to say letters.

One seems less alive, one digs in far from them, who are outside, on the surface, who hold the key to this set of acts.

One extracts fragments of a sequence, by chance.

In fact. Not by chance.

One arranges them, tries them out, ties them down.

Until in turn one holds the key.

Until in turn they hold up well together.

33. De la rigueur qui tourne, qui médite et qui chante.

Pas de ressassement. Des inflexions et des refrains.

Plutôt la phrase que le vers.

Livrée au mouvement mais dépendante. Librement dépendante.

Que la course obtenue soit le texte.

Ponctuation, ôtée ou mise, habits qui couvrent ou qui découvrent.

On a besoin, ou pas, d'espace, on aime, ou pas, les blocs de mots.

Moi maintenant j'aime les blocs, la phrase de la prose, comme un champ clos, à l'intérieur de quoi, variations infimes.

On cale bien son rythme, on compte l'*e* muet, on compte avec.

On improvise pour être vrai.

Une histoire apparaît que le vers empêchait, on la laisse passer, par instants, par saccades.

On ne la laisse pas s'emparer de l'espace.

On aime bien les mots suspendus au silence, posés sur le silence.

Comme des notes, uniques, graves, qui donnent sens et forme aux masses.

33. Precision which turns, which ponders and which sings.

No rumination. Inflections and refrains.

The sentence rather than the line.

Delivered over to the movement but dependent. Freely dependent.

So that the race won will be the text.

Punctuation, deleted or in place, garments that cover or uncover.

One needs, or doesn't need space, one likes, or not, the blocks of words.

As for me now I like the blocks, the prose sentence, like an enclosed field, and minute variations within it.

One props up the rhythm well, one counts the silent *e*, scans with it.

One improvises to be truthful.

A story appears that the verse impeded, one lets it pass, by moments, by jolts and starts.

One doesn't let it seize the space.

One likes words suspended from silence, set on silence.

Like notes, grave, solitary, which give sense and form to the masses.

34. Un témoin disparaît

34. A Witness Disappears

35. Plus elle parlait, plus ça s'obscurcissait.

Elle s'enfonçait dans la forêt partout et elle voyait la mer.

Occupée à tenir mes pensées je ne peux pas penser, je ne peux pas non plus empêcher les images.

— Dégorgeoir pour les huîtres.

« On les sort de la mer et on les met dans des bassins, qu'elles soient moins naturelles. »

Il lui avait porté un coup.

Elle était restée seule en compagnie de sa blessure, ne voulant pas mourir.

— Un port qu'on désensable.

« Les animaux, il n'y a rien à faire qu'à les manger. Le pire serait de les jeter.

« Les pierres, c'est différent, quand elles sont enlevées à la terre ou au sable, elles perdent leurs couleurs, il n'y a plus qu'à les jeter. »

Elle connaît le tableau sans l'avoir jamais vu.

Le blessé amené sur la plage, assis dans un fauteuil, dos à la mer, au spectateur. Le peloton de face.

— On avait nettoyé sa maison. Tout conservé intact.

Traversée de la peau.

Traversée de la peau.

35. The more she spoke, the darker it became.

She plunged into the forest everywhere and she saw the sea.

Busy holding on to my thoughts, I can't think, nor can I prevent the images.

— Oyster disgorger.

"They take them out of the sea and put them in basins, so that they will be less natural."

He had struck her.

She had remained alone in the company of her wound, not wishing to die.

— A port being cleared of sand.

"As for the animals, there's nothing to do but eat them. The worst thing would be to throw them away.

"Stones, that's different, when they're taken out of the earth or the sand, they lose their colors, there's nothing to do but throw them away."

She knew the picture without ever having seen it.

The wounded man brought to the beach, seated in an armchair, his back to the sea, to the spectator. Facing the firing squad.

— His house was cleaned. Everything left intact.

Crossing of the skin.

Crossing of the skin.

36. Mettre des talons hauts, une jupe fendue, se maquiller, pour aller dans la dune.

Image du renoncement.

Se lever, s'habiller pour aller voir la boîte aux lettres.

N'y trouver qu'une carte postale : le monument aux morts de son village.

Colle, ciseaux, épingles.

Ce n'est pas le procès que tu dis.

Le désir, trop énorme.

Je ne suis pas assez terrestre.

Souffrante, si.

Je suis venue ici avec le prince Muichkine. Et une angoisse : où est la boîte aux lettres ?

Il avait dit :

— Tu verras les oiseaux. Salue-les de ma part.

Pourquoi vivre à tout prix ? Pourquoi, une fois né, continuer à tout prix ?

Je salue les oiseaux de sa part. Ce sont des tournepierres, de petits échassiers.

36. To put on high heels, a slit skirt, to put on makeup, in order to go out on the dune.

Image of renunciation.

To get up, to get dressed, in order to check the mailbox.

To find there only a postcard: his village's monument to the war dead.

Glue, scissors, pins.

That's not the accusation you meant.

Desire, too enormous.

I am not earthly enough.

In pain, yes.

I came here with Prince Myshkin. And one concern: where is the mailbox?

He had said:

— You will see the birds. Greet them for me.

Why live at any price? Why, once born, continue at any price?

I greet the birds for him. They are turnstones, little sandpipers.

37. « Elle n'avait plus personne qu'elle-même : c'était mieux. »

Les maisons du pays étaient plates et basses. On aurait cru qu'on n'y pouvait tenir qu'assis.

On découvrait celle du peintre peu après le village, au début du marais.

La terre, le ciel, à cet endroit se marient bien.

La mer n'est pas très loin.

On s'y promènera le lendemain, les jours suivants.

On ira à Saint-Gilles-Croix-de-Vie et au port de l'Époids.

On ira là et là, je ne me souviens pas de tous les lieux précisément mais des dunes, des plages.

Et des photographies devant l'église.

Saint-Nicolas-de-Brem.

La maison est finie mais le ciment encore humide. J'ai l'impression.

Le peintre allume un feu de cheminée, il est penché, de dos.

Ce jour-là ou un autre, il m'offre un petit livre, imprimé au Japon, *Cent phrases pour éventails,* de Paul Claudel.

Je vois la cour et l'atelier. La maison est carrée, le jardin au milieu.

37. "She had no one but herself: it was better."

The houses of that country were low and flat. You'd have thought you could only stay in them sitting down.

The painter's house could be found a bit outside the village, at the edge of the swamp.

Earth and sky go well together there.

The sea is not too far away.

We'll go walking there the next day, the days after.

We'll go to Saint-Gilles-Croix-de-Vie and to the port at l'Époids.

We'll go here and there, I don't remember all the spots precisely, but dunes and beaches.

And photographs in front of the church.

Saint-Nicolas-de-Brem.

The house is finished but the cement is still wet. It seems to me.

The painter lights a fire in the fireplace, he is bent over, seen from behind.

That day, or another, he gives me a little book, printed in Japan, *One Hundred Sentences to Write on Fans* by Paul Claudel.

I see the courtyard and the studio. The house is square, the garden in the middle.

38. On me raconte : il pend ses toiles dans le soleil et dans le vent.

Il se promène au bord de l'eau, il recueille des traces sur des morceaux d'étoffes.

Celles des rochers, du paysage. Mais pas du vent, ni de l'espace, ni de la transparence, qu'il fera exister autrement.

Ses supports sont fragiles et précaires.

Ou destinés à autre chose.

Papier à lettres commercial, voilage de fenêtre ou toile à matelas.

Comme si le beau l'intimidait.

Plus tard.

Le bois présent dans la maison, la mort présente et nettoyée.

La femme parle d'une autre mort dans une autre maison où le bois est absent.

Bois des armoires où sont rangées les grandes toiles reprisées.

Assemblées et cousues.

Les zigzags de couleurs, quand le tissu était trop fin, ont fixé la peinture sur un tissu solide.

Dessins des points superposés à ceux du peintre.

38. I'm told: he hangs his canvases in the sun and in the wind.

He walks along the water's edge; he gathers traces on bits of fabric.

Of rocks, of the landscape. But not of the wind, nor of space, nor of transparency, that he will bring into being in other ways.

His surfaces are fragile and precarious.

Or meant for something else.

Commercial stationery, window-curtains, mattress ticking.

As if beauty intimidated him.

Later.

Wood that's present in the house, death present, cleaned off.

The woman speaks of another death in another house where wood is absent.

Wood of the armoires where the big mended canvases are stored.

Assembled and sewed.

The zigzags of color, when the fabric was too fine, fixed the paint onto a sturdier fabric.

Drawings made of dots, superimposed on the painter's.

39. Avant la nuit tombée, on descend les peintures de l'armoire, on les déploie sur les carreaux.

Les toiles lancent leurs couleurs, à nos yeux grands ouverts dans le noir.

Je me souviens de ses cheveux, longs et bouclés, de son sourire, son attention.

Tout à coup on pensait : il est là. Si présent.

Il épluchait les pommes de terre pour le repas : — Tu vois, si elles sont un peu vertes, elles te feront du mal.

Il prenait soin.

Un grand pays inexploré.

Je vois les tables, les objets. L'entassement.

Repas le soir. Chacun a voyagé. Moi plus que tous. Je ne dis rien et je m'ennuie. Il me sourit.

Dehors, le paysage est assombri sur le marais Mauvais, le marais Haut, le marais Braud, Rouaud, Guilbaud.

Le port aussi, c'est marée basse, l'eau de la mer s'est retirée, abandonnant la terre qui luit, dans le soleil couchant.

Les amas de varech, les trous où stagne l'eau, les bancs de sable sont fictifs.

La lumière vient du large, on lui tourne le dos, on voit le port à contre-jour, la terre imbibée d'eau et la mer en allée.

Au loin, au bout, les maisons basses et comme inhabitées.

39. Before nightfall, the paintings are taken out of the armoire, spread out on the tiles.

The canvases fire off their colors, to our eyes wide open in the darkness.

I remember his hair, long and curly, his smile, his attentiveness.

Suddenly you would think: he is here. So present.

He peeled potatoes for the meal: — You know, if they are a bit green, they'll make you ill.

He took care.

A large unexplored country.

I see the tables, the objects. The piling up.

The evening meal. Everyone has traveled. I more than anyone. I don't say anything and I get bored. He smiles at me.

Outside, the view has darkened on the Mauvais swamp, on the Haut swamp, the Braud, Rouaud, Guilbaud swamps.

At the port, too, it's low tide, the sea water has retreated, abandoning the earth that glows, in the setting sun.

The masses of kelp, the holes where water stagnates, the sandbars, are fictitious.

The light comes from the open sea, we turn our backs on it, we see the port backlit, the water-soaked earth and the sea gone away.

Far away, in the distance, the low houses, as if uninhabited.

40. Il peint sur papier kraft, papier canson, papier journal. Papier huilé, gouaché, gratté.

Il peint sur verre, panneau, particule de carton. Toile libre, métisse, légère, à matelas.

Avec de la peinture à l'huile. Vinyl, lavis, teinture. Crayon, pastel, encre de Chine. Encre d'imprimerie ou de stylo. Et aquarelle.

Par frottage, par froissage, par grattage, avec cutter, caillou, avec ongle, allumette.

Il peint des paysages à différents moments du jour.

Il a besoin de solitude.

Dans ce cas seulement les pommiers, les enfants, les rochers, les murettes se déforment, divaguent, non pas en proie au fantastique mais au réel, auquel il se soumet.

Le châssis a marqué la toile d'une croix.

La toile a un défaut.

Une goutte a coulé, et soudain, toute une armée de gouttes ont besoin de couler, il faut les projeter.

Il peint ou il écrit rapidement, habité par l'urgence, il saisit par surprise le tableau ou le texte, il se bat avec eux, l'image surgit par en dessous.

Il ne l'attendait pas.

Le peintre est seul à regarder. Quand il ferme les yeux, un témoin disparaît.

C'était lui, le dernier.

40. He paints on brown wrapping paper, Canson paper, newspaper. Paper that's been oiled, gouached, scratched.

He paints on glass, panel, pieces of cardboard. Free, hybrid, light canvas, mattress ticking.

With oil paints. Vinyl, wash drawing, dye. Pencil, pastel, India ink. Printers' ink or ink for pens. And watercolors.

By rubbing, creasing, scratching, with cutter, pebble, with fingernail, matchstick.

He paints landscapes at different times of day.

He needs solitude.

Only in this case do apple trees, children, rocks, low stone walls, become deformed, delirious, not in the grip of the fantastic, but of the real, to which he submits.

The stretchers have marked the canvas with a cross.

The canvas has a flaw.

A drop ran down, and suddenly, an army of drops need to run, they must be hurled.

He paints or he writes quickly, inhabited by urgency, he takes the picture or the text by surprise, he battles with them, the image springs up from below.

He wasn't expecting it.

The painter is the only one who looks. When he closes his eyes, a witness disappears.

It was he, the last one.

41. Impossible regard.

J'ai beau tenter, danseuse, de déplacer ma tête sur la droite ou la gauche de mon cou, rien n'y fait.

Je ne puis me jeter le coup d'oeil appuyé ou distrait qui me serait utile, que dis-je, indispensable pour me considérer de face.

Sans mimer fortement la grandeur.

Dehors la route était fermée, des milliers de papiers la couvraient.

Eux-mêmes étaient couverts par des milliers de mots.

Attroupement. Badauds. Gendarmes.

Un chauffeur de poids lourds était pris, un feuillet à la main.

Coupable !

Il se taisait et moi aussi.

Occupée que j'étais dans les jardins près du palais à sonder les sous-sols.

Criant :

— De l'eau, je veux de l'eau !

Personne n'écoutait.

41. Impossible gaze.

In vain do I, dancer, try to shift my head to the right or the left of my neck, it does no good.

I can't cast the insistent or distracted glance at myself that would be useful, what am I saying, indispensable, to stare at myself face to face.

Without overwhelmingly miming grandeur.

Outside the road was closed, thousands of papers covered it.

Themselves covered by thousands of words.

Crowd. Onlookers. Police.

A truck driver was arrested, a paper in his hand.

Guilty!

He was silent and so was I.

Busy as I was in the gardens near the palace sounding the depths of the basements.

Crying out:

— Water! I want water!

No one was listening.

42. Un passant me jeta, dédaigneux.

— L'eau de la terre ici est rare. On ne peut pas la cultiver.

Et du menton me désigna, protégé par des grilles et un gardien au torse nu, debout, les bras croisés, juste un jet recourbé comme un sexe fléchi.

— Que faites-vous ? me demanda un policier.

— Vous voyez bien que je travaille.

— C'est interdit ici.

— Je veux dire que je lis.

— Alors c'est différent.

Le policier se mit à rire et il m'apprit à devenir un cerf-volant.

Je m'envolais mais il tenait le fil, je restais accrochée à la terre, je ne me perdais pas en l'air.

Le policier revint souvent et moi aussi, ça me changeait de l'intérieur, où j'étais seule entre les murs.

Et où pourtant je percevais, quand je tendais l'oreille, la cohue d'une foule au travail.

Je circulais de pièce en pièce, inoccupées, je découvrais une photographie, c'était celle d'un homme qui avait gouverné autrefois le palais.

Qui s'était pris dans un miroir. L'appareil remplaçait le visage, il était le visage.

42. A passerby snapped at me, disdainfully:

— Water from the earth is rare here. It can't be cultivated.

And with his chin pointed out to me, protected by iron gates and a bare-chested guardian standing, naked to the waist, his arms crossed, a small curved jet, like a bent penis.

— What are you doing? a policeman asked me.

— You can see that I'm working.

— That's not permitted here.

— I meant to say that I'm reading.

— That's different.

The policeman burst out laughing and he taught me to become a kite.

I flew off, but he held the string, I remained tied to the earth, I didn't lose myself in the air.

The policeman came back often and so did I, it was a change for me from indoors, where I was alone between the walls.

And where nonetheless I sensed, when I lent an ear to it, the bustle of a crowd at work.

I roamed from room to room, all empty, I found a photograph, it was of a man who had governed the palace in former days.

Who had taken it of himself in a mirror. The camera replaced the face, it was the face.

43. Je pensais pour lutter : je suis Ang, je sais ce que je fais, ce que je suis, ce que je vaux.

C'était l'hiver, même dedans, les murs, le sol étaient glacés, les entrées et sorties dangereuses.

Un jour, je m'en souviens, je traversais le hall, je vis un homme près de la porte automatique.

Sa tête était coiffée d'un casque de mineur, surmonté d'une lampe.

Un éclair en jaillit, je me crus découpée en deux morceaux amers.

Ou foudroyée car située juste à l'intersection de l'énergie photographique qui interdit le mouvement et de la magnétique qui le permet.

Tous les combats ne sont pas bons, je le savais.

Mais le savoir n'arrangeait rien.

J'empruntais une porte discrète, descendais quelques marches et trouvais un taxi.

Quand j'arrivai chez moi le chauffeur me tendit de l'argent.

— Deux cent cinquante francs.

C'était lui qui payait.

La foule entrait dans le métro, descendait, s'enfonçait, comme bue par la terre.

De mon côté j'entrais chez moi, dans le couloir.

43. In order to maintain the struggle, I thought: I am Ang, I know what I am doing, what I am, what I'm worth.

It was winter, even indoors, the walls, the floor, were frozen, the entrances and exits dangerous.

One day, I remember, I was crossing the hall. I saw a man near the automatic door.

On his head was a miner's helmet, with a lamp atop it.

A light shone out of it, I thought I was cut into two bitter pieces.

Or struck by lightning since I was just at the intersection of photographic energy that prevents movement and magnetic energy which permits it.

Not every battle is worthwhile, I knew that.

But knowing it settled nothing.

I went out through an unobtrusive door, down a few steps, and found a taxi.

When I arrived home the driver proffered money to me.

— Two hundred and fifty francs.

It was he who paid.

The crowd entered the subway, descended, sank into it as if drunk by the earth.

As for me, I went into my house, into the hallway.

44. Il ne faut pas s'apitoyer sinon ce sentiment prendrait toute la place et alors, que d'ennui.

Je pensais : en effet.

Je montais un étage, deux étages, trois étages.

J'atteignais le sixième, je logeais sur les toits, je voyais la journée la blancheur de Montmartre et la nuit les lumières qui veillaient.

Dans la chambre d'en face, vivait un couple d'étrangers, des Yougoslaves.

La femme parlait fort, et même elle criait. Était-elle en colère ?

Lui ne répondait rien, jamais. Pourtant, je savais qu'il était avec elle, dans la pièce.

J'imaginais son corps, massif et brun, en face d'elle, assis, séparé par la table.

Je l'avais vu un jour, il marchait sur le toit en costume élégant et chaussures cirées.

Il longeait la gouttière, il atteignait sa chambre, ce soir-là sans lumière, il y disparaissait.

La nuit suivante, j'apercevais sa silhouette, cette fois éclairée par la lune, elle avançait vers ma fenêtre.

Elle avançait jusqu'à masquer le ciel, éclairé du dedans, la lune, quelques nuages.

Jusqu'à produire l'obscurité.

C'est entendu, ne vous répétez pas, je l'ai compris depuis longtemps : on confond innocent et coupable.

44. One must not feel sorry for oneself, or that sentiment will replace everything, and then, what a bore.

I thought: indeed.

I went up one story, two stories, three stories.

I reached the sixth floor, my window beneath the roof, during the day I saw the whiteness of Montmartre and at night the lights that kept watch.

In the room facing mine lived a couple of foreigners, Yugoslavians.

The woman spoke loudly, in fact, she shouted. Was she angry?

He never answered, not a word. And yet I knew that he was with her, in the room.

I imagined his body, massive and brown, facing her, seated, separated by the table.

I had seen him one day, he was walking on the roof in an elegant suit and polished shoes.

He walked alongside the drainpipe, he reached his room, unlit that night, he disappeared inside.

The following night, I saw his silhouette, this time lit by the moon, it was coming toward my window.

It came forward till it blocked out the sky, lit from within, the moon, a few clouds.

Until darkness ensued.

It's understood, don't repeat yourself, I've known it for a long time: one confuses the innocent with the guilty.

45. Dénégation de l'assassin

45. The Assassin's Denial

46. Lam entouré de nuit.

Il connaît vaguement son chemin, la porte en face, qui donne accès à un ponton.

L'ouvrir, sortir.

Lam incertain.

Quel est son bord de nuit, de quelle obscurité fera-t-il son chemin ?

Les raffales, dehors, font trembler le ponton, lui recule, je suis seul, il cherche à refermer la porte qui résiste.

Il rassemble son corps, décide de pousser, au moins de maintenir, épaule contre bois.

Du côté de la nuit, exactement derrière, une autre épaule pousse. Celle du vent ?

Parfois il tombe, alors plus rien ne se ressemble, c'est l'effroi sans couleur.

Pour tenir il se couche et se couvre beaucoup, il se protège avec du poids car trop léger et plat : une feuille qui a froid.

Parfois il s'accélère. À l'extérieur il est semblable.

A l'intérieur il se transforme en particules, qui remuent en tous sens.

Le désordre est affreux.

Il n'y a pas de vraies recettes pour guérir de l'effroi, même parler ne suffit pas.

46. Lam surrounded by night.

He knows his way vaguely, the door that faces him, opening onto a jetty.

Open it, go out.

Lam is uncertain.

Which edge of night is his, with what darkness will he make his way?

Gusts of wind, outside, make the jetty tremble, he draws back, I am alone, he tries to close the door again but it resists.

He tenses his body, decides to push, at least to hold fast, shoulder against wood.

On the night side, exactly opposite, another shoulder pushes back. The wind's?

Sometimes he falls, then nothing makes sense, it is colorless dread.

To hold out he lies down and covers himself amply, he protects himself with weight because he is too light and flat, a chilly leaf.

Sometimes he speeds up. Outside, he's the same.

Inside he breaks into particles that shift in every direction.

The disorder is frightful.

There are no real remedies to cure dread, even to speak of it is not enough.

47. Lam entouré de jour.

La mer s'étend et l'air circule.

Les estivants n'ont pas de chambres, encore moins des maisons, mais des couchettes, superposées, dans une construction en métal peint de gris.

Ce n'est pas un bateau ou alors immobile, ensablé.

Pour se rendre à la plage, Lam traverse le dortoir, en empruntant la voie étroite qui sépare les couchettes.

Un matin il entend haleter.

L'homme est massif, allongé sur le dos, le regard vers le ciel de la couchette du dessus, l'expression concentrée.

Lam marche vite, pressé de laisser l'homme, il est pris d'un dégoût qu'il ne s'explique pas.

Le soir il va dîner chez une amie célibataire. L'appartement est au sixième, l'immeuble est vieux.

Il monte l'escalier récemment restauré, les marches, couvertes de tommettes, sont bordées de bois clair.

La rampe est peinte en bleu.

— À ta place j'aurais peur, la maison est fragile, l'escalier suspendu. Comment tiennent les marches ?

Par la fenêtre en face, ouverte sur l'été, il aperçoit des plantes vertes, un canapé.

L'appartement est vide.

47. Lam surrounded by day.

The sea stretches out and the air circulates.

The summer residents don't have rooms, certainly not houses, but bunks, one on top of another, in a gray-painted metal edifice.

It is not a boat, or it is an immobile one, stuck in the sand.

To get to the beach, Lam crosses the dormitory, taking the narrow corridor between the bunks.

One morning he hears panting.

The man is massive, lying on his back, staring at the sky of the bunk above, his expression concentrated.

Lam walks quickly, hurrying to leave the man behind, he is seized by an inexplicable disgust.

In the evening he has dinner with an unmarried woman friend. Her apartment is on the sixth floor, the building is old.

He goes up the recently restored staircase, the steps, covered in red clay tile, are bordered with light colored wood.

The banister is painted blue.

— In your place, I'd be afraid, the building is fragile, the stairway suspended. How do the steps stay in place?

Through the window across the way, open on summer, he sees green plants, a couch.

The apartment is empty.

48. Maison à un étage.

Lam et sa femme dorment en haut.

Ils ont tort car en bas la porte reste ouverte pour des hordes qui passent.

Le lendemain sur le trottoir, au pied de leur perron, ils trouvent père et soeur assommés dans la nuit.

Lam accuse sa femme : qui sinon elle est la gardienne ?

Pendant ce temps, la porte reste ouverte pour l'inconnu qui entre et rôde.

C'est l'assommeur. Que cherche-t-il ?

Dehors, un couple passe : — On se retrouve quand ?

Deux femmes en pantouffles :

— Ça va le chien ?

— Il est dans la fontaine, il prend son bain.

La rue compense l'affreux désordre du dedans.

Le malheur, pense Lam, n'est jamais qu'un rond jaune sur le sol de la scène.

Pour sortir, faire un pas de côté.

48. A two-story house.

Lam and his wife sleep upstairs.

They shouldn't, because the ground floor door stays open to the passing hordes.

The next day on the sidewalk, at the foot of the stairs, they find father and sister felled during the night.

Lam accuses his wife: who if not she is the janitor?

During this time, the door remains open for a stranger who comes in and prowls around.

It is the assailant. What is he looking for?

Outside, a couple passes by: — When will we see each other again?

Two women in bedroom slippers:

— How's the dog?

— He's in the fountain, he's having his bath.

The street makes up for the frightful mess within.

Misfortune, thinks Lam, is nothing but a yellow spotlight on the stage floor.

To exit, take a step aside.

49. Le voisin chante.

— J'ai pas tué ma mère, j'ai pas tué ma soeur.

Moi non plus, pense Lam.

Dénégation de l'assassin.

La voisine époussette. Les pots de fleurs n'ont pas de fleurs, sur le rebord de la fenêtre.

Les gens sont drôles, pense Lam.

Au repas, il raconte :

— En sortant du métro, à trois pas devant moi, un aveugle, qu'un Africain bouscule pour venir droit sur moi.

« Quatre femmes m'ont battu, me dit-il.

« Ses yeux sont rouges, comme s'il avait pleuré, ou bu. Il me poursuit en répétant, quatre femmes m'ont battu. »

Le père écoute, il mange, la poudre qu'il avale déborde de sa bouche, en mousse jaune.

Le récit de la mère n'a ni début ni fin.

— Elle s'appelait Douleur. C'est son mari qui le disait.

Paix dans les mots. La paix aux mots.

49. The man next door is singing.

— Didn't kill my mother, didn't kill my sister.

Me neither, thinks Lam.

The assassin's denial.

The woman next door is dusting. There are no flowers in the flowerpots on the windowsill.

People are peculiar, thinks Lam.

During dinner, he says:

— Coming out of the subway, three steps ahead of me, a blind man, whom an African shoved aside to get close to me.

"Four women beat me up, he said to me.

"His eyes were red, as if he had been crying, or drinking. He followed me repeating, four women beat me up."

The father listens, he eats, the powder that he's swallowing oozes from his mouth in yellow foam.

The mother's story has neither start nor finish.

— She was called Sorrow. It was her husband who said so.

Peace in the words. Peace to the words.

50. Le décor change constamment.

Pour aller vite et simplifier, le figurer pas des photos projetées sur un mur.

L'annoncer chaque fois de la sorte :

Je m'en vais en Annam, je m'en vais au Tonkin, je m'en vais en Afrique.

La voix est une, bien que multiple.

Sur les photos des vues d'ensemble, mais aussi des détails, des objets sans valeurs.

Un livre déchiré dont on voit une image, des pierres disposées, des bassines de fleurs, des plantes grasses, un banc.

Un chemin dans les pins, la plage, un paquebot, une rue en Asie, des enfants qui se battent.

La liste continue. L'organiser et l'augmenter mais avec précaution, dissimuler l'intime, ne révéler que le visible, des objets et des lieux décrochés, autonomes.

Conversation des âmes soeurs.

De quoi viendra l'action ?

De femmes attendues, arrivées, reparties, qu'on ne voit pas, qu'on n'a pas vues.

Il faut qu'on se soupçonne et qu'on s'accuse.

Elles étaient là pourtant mais j'ai tourné la tête et hop !

50. The scene is constantly changing.

To go quickly and simplify, indicate it by photos projected on a wall.

Announce it each time saying:

Now I am going to Annam, now I am going to Tonkin, now I am going to Africa.

There is only one voice, although it is multiple.

In the photos, general views, but also details, insignificant objects.

A torn book in which one sees a picture, carefully placed stones, bowls of flowers, succulents, a bench.

A path amidst the pines, the beach, an ocean liner, a street in Asia, children fighting.

The list continues. Organize it and add to it, but with caution, dissimulate the intimate, reveal only the visible, disconnected objects and places, autonomous.

Conversation of kindred spirits.

Where will the action come from?

From women who are expected, arrive, leave again, whom one does not see, whom one has not seen.

Mutual suspicion and accusation are necessary.

Still, they were there but I turned my eyes away and presto!

51. « Nos frères nous calomnièrent, ils forment contre nous d'injustes prétentions, confondant l'innocence et le crime. »

De son séjour dans l'assemblée du monde, Lam ramena des discordances.

Conditions d'admission.

La loi n'est pas écrite, avec le temps on la devine, on se dépouille, on ne conserve que sa peau, qu'on met dehors-dedans.

Ainsi va-t-on sans contenu, contenant à l'envers. On a tourné.

Conditions d'existence.

On en prend l'habitude, on tient debout tenu aux actes, à quoi on est porté sans cesse.

L'événement approche, l'excuse de l'urgence fait remettre à plus tard le soin de revenir à soi, de s'habiter au moins un peu.

On est interchangeable, on n'a pas de repli, on est roulé, jeté au fond, puis remonté.

Tout de même on essaie de garder quelque chose.

Résolution.

Élucider l'alternative : dehors ? dedans ?

Les animaux volants sont attirés, dans les lieux clos, par les hauteurs.

Ils montent, cherchant en vain une ouverture, qui est au sol.

51. "Our brothers slandered us, they make unjust claims against us, confusing innocence and guilt."

From his sojourn at the world's assembly, Lam brought back disagreements.

Conditions of admission.

The law is not written down, in time one guesses it, divests oneself of it, one keeps only one's skin, which one turns inside out.

Thus one goes on with no contents, containing the wrong way round. One has turned.

Conditions of existence.

One gets the habit of it, one remains standing, held to one's actions, to which one is constantly referred.

The event approaches, the excuse of urgency makes one delay the task of returning to oneself, inhabiting oneself at least a bit.

One is interchangeable, one has nowhere to retreat, one is rolled up, thrown to the bottom, then raised up again.

One tries to hold on to something all the same.

Resolution.

Clarify the alternative: Outside? Inside?

Flying animals, in enclosed spaces, are attracted by the heights.

They climb, looking in vain for an opening, which is on the ground.

52. *Le plus petit que le petit.*

Il se met un bonnet, deux bonnets, trois bonnets.

Il se met des lunettes.

N'entend pas.

Il entend seulement après appels réitérés.

Il est collé à son dossier, ne bouge pas.

Ne bouge pas !

Le commis principal.

Il est assis à son bureau, il avance des mots, de plus en plus de mots, qui deviennent un mur.

Quel était le propos ?

Lam ne s'en souvient plus.

Le commis principal est la loi, à tout le moins son porte-enseigne.

— Voyons, voyons, que puis-je pour vous ?

Comme il se plaît quand il est bon !

52. The smaller than small.

He puts on a bonnet, two bonnets, three bonnets.

He puts on glasses.

Doesn't hear.

He hears only after repeated calls.

He's glued to his case file, doesn't move.

Don't move!

The principal agent.

He is seated at his desk, he pushes words forward, more and more words, till they become a wall.

What was the subject?

Lam doesn't remember.

The principal agent is the law, or at least its standard-bearer.

— Now, now, what can I do for you?

How pleased he is when he is good!

53. La future concubine.

Elle dit qu'elle a fait ça et ça, qu'elle est trop bonne, qu'elle rend service.

Elle relève sa mèche, elle est charmante, elle entre.

Ainsi elle entre.

Elle fait des tas qu'elle utilise ou qu'elle remise, suivant le cours, sentant le vent.

Elle tient du canotier ou de la blatte. Elle est très plate.

Technique de pointe.

On met quelqu'un en l'air, il reste suspendu.

Tout le monde est requis pour donner son avis.

Ceux qui sont déjà là et les nouveaux et ceux qui passent, afin de ne manquer en aucun cas la vérité.

On ne la manque pas, on vise bien, on tue.

L'assemblée se désole.

— Pour sûr, nous l'aimions bien !

Pendant ce temps le jour d'hiver est gai.

53. *The future concubine.*

She says that she has done this and that, and that she is too kind, that she helps out.

She brushes her bangs aside, she is charming, she enters.

Thus she enters.

She makes little piles that she uses or puts away, following the flow, sniffing the wind.

She's something like a straw hat or a cockroach. She's very flat.

How to press a point.

Someone is hoisted in the air, he hangs there.

Everyone is asked to give an opinion.

Those who are already there, and newcomers, and the passers-by, so as not to miss the truth by any means.

One does not miss, one aims well, one kills.

The audience is sorry.

— For sure, we were very fond of him.

All this time, the winter day is gay.

54. La fin du jour.

À un étage, dans un bureau ensoleillé (le mur est une vitre), l'employé est tombé en avant, sur le visage et sur la table, dans ses dossiers.

Comme une feuille détachée.

Évènement.

On est dans son bureau.

Les actes sont dressés comme des arbres dans le jour.

Il faut en choisir un, pour commencer.

Ensuite organiser un ordre de passage.

Mais on ne bouge pas.

C'est une indifférence qui survient, c'est une suspension, c'est une suspicion, accusation, condamnation.

C'est une erreur !

On est dressé.

— C'est une erreur !

Mais où sont-ils ?

54. The end of the day.

On one floor, in a sunlit office (one wall is a pane of glass) the employee has fallen forward, on his face and on the table, head in his files.

Like a fallen leaf.

Event.

One is in the office.

The acts stand erect like trees in the daylight.

One of them must be chosen, to begin.

Then organize an order of passage.

But no one moves.

An indifference arises, there's a suspension, there's a suspicion, accusation, condemnation.

It's a mistake.

One protests.

— It's a mistake!

But where are they?

55. *Sursaut.*

Réfléchir et comprendre et convaincre.

Fléchir et prendre et vaincre ? Les mots sont drôles.

L'ordonnateur :

— Tout va très bien, je pense à toi.

Puis il passe, impatient, enfin aux vrais sujets, à ses difficultés, à comment va le monde.

Poser le front contre le meuble et demander à soi, comme si n'étaient rien tant d'années au combat :

— Est-ce possible ?

Tandis que la rumeur circule, qu'elle anticipe.

Départ.

On a posé le pied sur l'ombre d'une marche. On tombe.

L'escalier est de marbre.

Délectation.

On se dérobe c'est la nuit.

55. Sudden start.

To reflect and understand and convince.

To flex and stand and vanquish? Words are peculiar.

The organizer:

— Everything's fine, I'm thinking of you.

Then, impatient, he gets to his real subjects, to his problems, what's going on in the world.

Put your forehead against the piece of furniture and ask yourself, as if so many years of struggle were for nothing:

— Is it possible?

While the rumour goes around, anticipates.

Departure.

You've put your foot on the shadow of a step. You fall.

The staircase is marble.

Delight.

You draw back, it's night.

56. Veilleur qui réfléchit

56. Watchman, Reflecting

57. Lam a son peintre aussi, différent du premier, celui d'Ang.

Le sien vit en Bretagne, il n'a de lui que des dessins, qu'il pend au mur.

Il n'a que le regard du sourd.

Parfois le sourd n'a pas la vue, mais ce n'est pas son cas.

Lam a la vue à peu près bonne.

— Remercions le Seigneur.

Il se met à genoux.

Le Seigneur, en revanche, n'entend pas.

Trop de coton dans les oreilles.

Trop d'air, entre la terre et lui.

Entre lui et les arbres.

Entre lui, les oiseaux, les bateaux et les têtes.

Le feu qui rouge.

Ou plutôt qui s'exclame.

57. Lam, too, has his painter, different from the first one, Ang's.

His lives in Brittany, all Lam has of his is drawings, which he hangs on the wall.

All he has is the deaf man's glance.

Sometimes a deaf man can also not see, but that isn't the case here.

Lam has more or less good vision.

— Thank the Lord.

He goes down on his knees.

The Lord, on the other hand, does not hear.

Too much cotton in his ears.

Too much air, between the earth and himself.

Between him and the trees.

Between him, the birds, boats and heads.

The fire that reddens.

Or, rather, that cries out.

58. Parfois la vue console Lam.

C'est à cause des traits qui encadrent la tête.

La tête ne rit pas.

Elle est à la fenêtre et elle profère.

On ne sait pas bien quoi.

Des histoires, des injures, des admonestations ?

Ou encore des ?

Et des ?

Prières ?

La tête se déplace, d'abord à gauche et en hauteur.

Le plafond semble bas.

Ou c'est le front qui s'est tassé.

Les pensées s'amenuisent, menuisent.

Me nuisent.

58. Sometimes vision consoles Lam.
It's because of the pencil-strokes that frame the head.
The head does not laugh.
It's at the window and it utters.
One is not quite sure what.
Stories, insults, admonitions?
Or perhaps some . . . ?
And some?
Prayers?
The head moves about, first to the left and higher up.
The ceiling seems low.
Or it's the forehead that has crammed itself down.
Thoughts become inert, what they insert
Is meant to hurt.

59. En bas à droite, c'est le nez qui prétend cette fois opérer.

Lam veut dire : commander.

La tête crie des ordres en regardant le ciel.

La tête crie des ordres en regardant de face.

La bouche est de travers, presque en dessous de l'œil.

L'autre œil est blanc.

Il est fermé ou atrophié.

Le nez descend jusqu'au menton.

La tête est attrapée par le vertige.

Elle noircit et descend dans un coin.

Les sourcils ont grandi.

Le nez s'est dédoublé pour occuper tout le terrain.

La tête est bonne surveillante.

Nul n'en réchappera.

59. Lower down, to the right, it's the nose which, this time, claims to act.

Lam means: to command.

The head shouts orders while looking at the sky.

The head shouts orders while looking straight ahead.

The mouth is askew, almost right below the eye.

The other eye is white.

It is closed or atrophied.

The nose goes right down to the chin.

The head becomes dizzy.

It darkens and descends into a corner.

The eyebrows have thickened.

The nose has split in two to occupy the whole territory.

The head is a good guard.

No one will escape from it.

60. La tête est fatiguée.

Nez de pantin, coup de côté, la tête perd de la hauteur.

Une fois n'est pas coutume mais cette fois la fois est bonne.

La tête est arrangée, elle s'enfonce et crie, sous la fumée qui s'accumule.

Puis le corps a fini par sortir.

Il est assis en haut du cadre.

— Je vous écoute, dit-il.

Il fume.

Les deux yeux se rapprochent du nez.

Le corps se tourne à gauche.

Il est épais.

Il bouge d'un seul morceau, du crâne jusqu'aux pieds.

Le corps fait mine.

Il s'appuie en arrière sur les coudes.

60. The head is tired.

Puppet's nose, a blow on the side, the head loses altitude.

Just this once won't hurt, but this once, once was enough.

The head has straightened itself, it sinks and cries out, under the gathering smoke.

Then the body finally emerged.

It's seated on top of the frame.

— I'm listening to you, it says.

It's smoking.

The two eyes draw closer to the nose.

The body turns to the left.

It's thick.

It moves with one motion, from the skull to the feet.

The body strikes a pose.

It leans backward on its elbows.

61. Il se remet d'aplomb.

Les yeux deviennent noirs.

Le nez fend le visage en deux.

Il devient coi.

La bouche dit :

— Au feu ! Au feu !

Comme elle dirait voilà voilà !

D'autres mots, d'autres moeurs.

L'horizon prend le pas sur la mer, hors du cadre.

Pas plus inquiet que ça, le corps, disposé sur le mur, à surveiller la côte.

Et les bateaux.

Et les bébés langés dedans.

Les cheminées qui vont par trois.

Et les veilleurs.

61. It pulls itself upright.

The eyes turn black.

The nose cuts the face in two.

It is rendered speechless.

The mouth says:

— Fire! Fire!

As if it were saying, "There it is! There it is!"

Other words, other ways.

The horizon dominates the sea, beyond the frame.

No more uneasy than that, the body, laid out on the wall, to watch the coast.

And the boats.

And the babies swaddled within them.

The chimneys that go three by three.

And the watchmen.

62. Le corps est sur le mur, il surveille les veilleurs qui se tiennent les coudes.

Les veilleurs n'ont pas froid ni aux yeux ni ailleurs car ils sont très couverts.

Capuche et robe jusqu'en bas.

Juste des trous pour voir.

Parfois le sol est aussi noir que leurs habits.

Parfois l'un d'eux est blanc.

Et le chemin qui part devant, laiteux.

Parfois aucun veilleur n'est blanc.

Le plus gros au milieu explique quelque chose.

Ou réfléchit.

Car le chemin devenu noir en a croisé un autre.

Il dit :

— Voilà, voilà.

Ou il dit :

— Bon.

62. The body is on the wall, it is watching the watchmen who stand together.

The watchmen are not cold, not their eyes or anywhere else, since they are well covered up.

Hoods and robes down to the ground.

Just holes to see out of.

Sometimes the ground is as black as their clothing.

Sometimes one of them is white.

And the road that leads forward, milky.

Sometimes no watchman is white.

The heaviest one in the middle is explaining something.

Or thinking.

For the road turned black has crossed another one.

He says:

— There it is, there it is.

Or he says:

— Good.

63. Le corps est sur le mur, il surveille les gisants.

Pauvres corps attachés, roulés sur le côté.

Les têtes n'ont plus cours.

Les têtes sont des croix qui crient :

— À moi, à moi.

Il surveille les bateaux en gésine.

La mer est comme un mur, mais habitée par les poissons.

La cheminée est une chose rouge, dressée.

Les nuages vont tomber, la mer entrer dans la colère.

Mais le bateau est immuable.

L'effort le ronge mais pas le rouge.

Le rouge est immuable.

Les arbres se délectent à voir tomber la nuit dans l'eau, tantôt par ricochet et tantôt par défaut.

Eux sont aussi sereins que des totems.

63. The body is on the wall, it is watching the recumbent figures.

Poor trussed bodies, rolled onto their sides.

The heads are out of circulation.

The heads are crosses crying out:

— Here, to me! Here, to me!

It watches the boats in labor.

The sea is like a wall, but inhabited by fish.

The chimney is a red thing, erect.

The clouds will gather, the sea become enraged.

But the boat is immutable.

The effort gnaws at it but not the redness.

The redness is immutable.

The trees take pleasure seeing night fall on the water, sometimes indirectly and sometimes by default.

They are as serene as totem poles.

64. Le corps est sur le mur.

Il surveille les régentes.

Elles portent des lunettes noires.

Elles ne s'amusent pas.

Leurs mains sont sur la table pour bien montrer qu'elles ne font rien.

Devant le mur qui était rouge, qui devient bleu, bleu très foncé, leurs yeux sont des trous noirs.

Croix de bois croix de fer si je mens.

— Je ne mens pas, dit Lam.

« J'aime mieux regarder que d'habiter dans la passion. »

Il est content.

Plus rien ne le retient.

La bonne essuie ses mains au tablier.

Elle est nouvelle.

— Que se passe-t-il ? demande-t-elle.

64. The body is on the wall.

It watches the Queens Regent.

They are wearing dark glasses.

They are not amused.

Their hands are on the table to make it clear that they are doing nothing.

Before the wall, which was red, which is turning blue, very dark blue, their eyes are black holes.

Cross my heart and hope to die if I'm telling a lie.

— I'm not lying, says Lam.

"I'd rather look than live in passion."

He is satisfied.

Nothing more holds him back.

The maid wipes her hands on her apron.

She's new.

— What's going on? she asks.

65. Lam est tombé dans les dessins comme on tombe amoureux.

Il s'est mis à danser autour d'eux.

Danser avec les mots.

Les mots étaient sa danse.

La danse autour des corps muets.

Les dessins et les mots se contemplent.

Se contentent ?

Oui pourquoi pas ils sont contents les uns des autres.

On ne sait pas qui voit, qui surveille qui.

Lam, ou le corps sur le mur, ou le veilleur qui réfléchit ?

Le flambeau passe, du regardant au regardé qui regarde à son tour.

Certains mots font figure de témoin.

C'est le pays de fatrasie.

Lam est un roi sans commentaire, idiot blanchi par la farine, ange sans frères.

65. Lam fell into the drawings the way you fall in love.
He began to dance around them.
To dance with words.
Words were his dance.
The dance around mute bodies.
The drawings and the words gazed at each other.
Were satisfied with each other?
Yes why not they were satisfied with each other.
One does not know who sees, who watches whom.
Lam, or the body on the wall, or the watchman who reflects.
The torch passes, from the watcher to the watched who watched in his turn.
Certain words are regarded as witnesses.
It was the country of clutter.
Lam is a king who makes no remarks, flour-whitened idiot, brotherless angel.

66. Développer est superflu.

N'écrire que des notes, allées, venues de l'oeil, du souvenir.

Rencontrer le hasard.

Ne pas chercher la perfection dans le tracé exact, la reconstitution, ni le salut dans le détail, le luxe du réel.

Avoir de la patience, laisser flotter l'image.

D'abord le blanc, comme une tache claire, un trou : on y distingue un personnage, nommé par la lumière, en même temps qu'exclu du reste de l'image.

Les autres sont absents, la faute en est au photographe, accordé à ce blanc, cette fausse innocence.

L'homme donne le change, dans les gradins, parmi la foule, qui n'a d'yeux que pour lui et la course.

Qui parle de quoi ? De qui ?

De quoi de quoi ?

Je n'entends pas. Pouvez-vous répéter ? Avoir cette obligeance ?

Dans ce vacarme votre voix. Dans cette poix votre clameur.

Ah voilà qui est mieux.

Ils filent devant moi, je les regarde des tribunes, ils courent ils courent les chevaux, ils ont raison, c'est bien connu, seuls ils ont du génie.

66. Development is superfluous.

To write only notes, comings and goings of the eye, of memory.

To encounter chance.

Not to seek perfection in detail, in the perfect pencil-stroke, the re-creation, nor salvation in details, the luxury of the real.

To have patience, to let the image float.

The white first, like a pale stain, a hole: one can make out a human figure in it, named by the light while being excluded from the rest of the image.

The others are absent, it's the photographer's fault, tuned to this white, this false innocence.

The man is swindling them, there in the stadium, amidst the crowd that has eyes only for him and for the race.

Who is speaking of what? Of whom?

Of what of what?

I don't understand. Can you repeat? Would you be so kind?

In that din your voice. In that pitch your shouting.

Ah that's better.

They file in front of me, I watch them from the grand-stand, they run they run those horses, they're right, it's well known, on their own they are brilliant.

67. La fin et le commencement

67. The End and the Beginning

68. — Ah, commençons, dit Lam, je n'en peux plus
d'attendre.

Il montre le rideau :

— Allez, allez, relève-toi !

Il montre le plafond :

— Allez, allez, éclaire-toi, que la nuit se dissipe !

Il bat des mains :

— Le spectacle commence !

Il trépigne.

Dans le public, quelqu'un lève la main, c'est un jeune
homme austère, lunettes rondes, silhouette efflanquée.

— Pardonnez-moi, monsieur, mais je voudrais inter-
venir.

Lam l'interrompt :

— Commencez, je vous prie.

Le jeune homme se lance :

— C'est la fin qui précède et le début qui suit.

68. — Oh, let's get started, says Lam, I can't stand waiting anymore.

He points to the curtain:

— Go on, go on, rise!

He points to the ceiling:

— Go on, go on, light up, let the night vanish!

He claps his hands!

— The show is starting!

He stamps his feet.

In the audience, someone raises his hand, it's an austere young man, round spectacles, lanky.

— Excuse me, sir, but I'd like to say something.

Lam interrupts him:

— Get started, please!

The young man hazards:

— It's the end that precedes and the beginning which follows.

69. À côté une dame un peu forte remue la tête de haut en bas pour marquer son accord.

— Autrement dit, pour être, il faut avoir été.

Le jeune homme, encouragé par son élan de débutant et prenant l'assemblée à témoin :

— Si, si, ne vous étonnez pas.

Lam reprend la parole :

— On a beau dire, finir est bien, mais commencer est préférable.

Le jeune homme proteste :

— Finir est nostalgique et commencer est difficile.

Un homme entre deux âges.

— Il faut savoir finir avant de commencer.

Lam qui s'agace :

— Il faut bien commencer pour que le reste vienne.

— Commencer quoi et finir quoi ?

L'homme entre deux est dédaigneux.

69. Beside him, a rather stout lady shakes her head up and down to indicate her agreement.

— In other words, to be, one must have been.

The young man, stimulated by his beginner's momentum, and calling the audience to witness:

— Yes, yes, don't be surprised.

Lam speaks up again:

— Whatever one says, ending is good, but beginning is preferable.

The young man protests:

— Ending is nostalgic and beginning is difficult.

A middle-aged man:

— You've got to know how to end before beginning.

Lam, who's getting annoyed:

— You've still got to begin for the rest to follow.

— Begin what and end what?

The middle man is disdainful.

70. — Que me chantez-vous là, réplique Lam, pour moi . . .

— Qu'on en finisse, qu'on en finisse, interrompt le jeune homme.

— Ah, que vienne la fin, qu'on passe enfin à autre chose, soutient la dame mûre en s'éventant.

— Fini, fidi, fici, risque Lam, hésitant.

— La fin, pour moi, dit un vieillard en se grattant la nuque.

Lam avance le micro.

— La journée va finir et la nuit commencer.

Chacun retient son souffle, le ton est solemnel, le temps est à la prophétie.

— Puis la nuit va finir, la journée commencer.

« Moi je suis au milieu, dans ce creux, ce ressac, entre une fin et un commencement.

« À nouveau une fin.

« Courant de l'un à l'autre, hâtant la fin de l'un pour le début de l'autre.

« Soignant, oignant la fin de l'un pour la merveille, le panache de l'autre. »

Le vieillard fait la pause.

70. — What are you going on about, retorts Lam, as far as I'm concerned . . .

— Get it over with, get it over with, interrupts the young man.

— Ah, let the end come, and get on to something else, agrees the mature woman, fanning herself.

— Fini, fidi, fici, Lam dares, hesitant.

— The end, for me, says an old man, scratching the back of his neck.

Lam gives him the microphone.

— The day will end and the night begin.

Everyone holds his breath, the tone is solemn, and the hour ripe for prophecy.

— Then the night will end and the day begin.

"As for me, I am in the middle, in that hollow, that backwash, between an end and a beginning.

"Once more, an end.

"Running from one to the other, hastening the end of one so that the other can begin.

"Caring for, anointing the end of one for the marvel, the verve of the other."

The old man pauses.

71. — Ah cette fin du jour !

« Mais cette fin du jour est le début du soir.

« Je m'apprête à le boire, à pénétrer la soie du soir, avec les mouvements lents du dormeur, les mouvements de l'enveloppement sur soi, de l'immobilité apparente du rêve.

« Ou bien avec le frémir du veilleur qui s'élance. »

Chacun écoute le vieillard avec admiration.

Une femme encore belle, un peu jalouse du vieillard, prend la relève.

Dommage, pense le public, qui s'était attaché au vieillard et préférait sa suite à un commencement inattendu.

— Oui, tout est bon de ce qui vient si je sais m'y prêter, m'y apprêter, m'en caresser, m'en oindre, ah je ruisselle.

L'auditoire ne dit mot.

— Je n'en peux plus de ce qui est derrière.

« Mais je le tiens encore, je le tire jusqu'au bord de ce qui est devant, chargée et neuve et regardée tout à la fois par ces extrêmes et enchantée de les marier. »

Le public se rassure, il avait craint le pire.

Lam est content, la représentation se passe bien, elle suit son cours.

À présent engagée elle devrait s'en aller doucement vers sa fin.

71. — Ah, that ending of day!

"But that ending of day is the beginning of evening.

"I prepare myself to drink, to penetrate the silk of sun-down, with a sleeper's slow movements, movements of self-surrounding, of a dream's apparent immobility.

"Or perhaps with the shudder of a lookout rushing forward."

Everyone listens to the old man with admiration.

A still-beautiful woman, a bit envious of the old man, takes her turn.

What a pity, thinks the audience, grown attached to the old man and preferring his next utterance to an unexpected beginning.

— Yes, all that will come is for the best if I know how to yield to it, prepare for it, caress and anoint myself with it, ah, I'm overflowing.

The audience doesn't make a sound.

— I can no longer endure what's behind.

"But I still hold on to it, I pull it to the edge of what lies ahead, encumbered and new and observed all at once by these extremes and delighted to be combining them.

The public is reassured, it had feared the worst.

Lam is content, the performance is going well, it's running its course.

Well under way now, it ought to go smoothly toward its end.

72. La femme n'avait pas fini. Elle poursuit donc :

— Et juchée sur l'instant, cette crête, autre et même toujours.

Un professeur prend la parole avec autorité.

Il est clair qu'il s'apprête à conclure, à finir en beauté, entonner le meilleur pour la fin.

— On peut imaginer que non, qu'il n'y a pas.

Il marque un temps d'arrêt pour que chacun se pende à son discours.

— Qu'il n'y a pas de succession, de ces moutonnements dont nous avons parlé, pas de ressac, de recommencements.

« Mais une immense scène, un immense plateau où tout est déjà là.

« Toutes les fins, tous les débuts déjà posés dans l'ordre ou le désordre peu m'importe.

« On va de l'un à l'autre quitte à mourir avant de naître.

« On circule on choisit, on s'en va, on revient, présent à tout en même temps.

« Tout est donné en vrac.

« Pas seulement chaque instant d'une vie, mais chaque instant de toute vie.

« En sorte qu'on circule dans un lieu où le tien et le mien se mélangent, où j'appartiens à la poussière du temps. »

72. The woman hadn't finished. So she continues.

— And perched on the moment, this crest, forever other and the same.

A professor speaks up with authority.

It's evident that he is getting ready to conclude, to finish with a flourish, to intone the best part last.

— One can imagine that no, that there isn't.

He pauses so that everyone is hanging on his words.

— That there is no succession, to these frothings of which we've spoken, no backwash, no resumption.

"But a huge stage, a platform where all is already present.

"All the endings, all the beginnings, already set in order or disorder, what does it matter.

"One goes from one to the other, even if it means dying before being born.

"One circulates, one chooses, one goes away, one comes back, present to all at the same time.

"Everything is given at once.

"Not only each moment of a life, but each moment of every life.

"In such a way that one circulates in a space where yours and mine are mixed, where I belong to the dust of time."

73. Le public applaudit, le professur salue, la public applaudit, le professeur salue, le public applaudit, le professeur déjà debout, qui croyait la partie terminée, s'incline derechef.

Une donzelle nasille pour lui niquer sa pige.

Quelqu'un ricane. La donzelle est douteuse.

Non c'est elle qui doute :

— À quelle aurore dédier mon bras, mon dos, mon corps parfait ?

Protestations.

La donzelle minaude, un cornet d'ice-cream à la main, le nez chaussé de ses lunettes Lolita, tandis qu'Humpty-Dumpty la guette à quelques pas, bien décidé à la.

Musique !

La fanfare du matin retentit.

Dépêchons-nous !

Se lever, se langer, se jucher, s'arroger.

On entend les nouvelles.

— Trois jours pour éviter la guerre !

— Pourquoi trois jours ? s'étonne Lam en s'éveillant.

73. The audience applauds, the professor takes a bow, the audience applauds, the professor takes a bow, the audience applauds, the professor, already standing, who thought the match was over, bends forward once again.

A nasal damsel pipes up to swipe his pittance.

Someone snickers. The damsel is dubious.

No, it's she who doubts:

— To what dawn shall I dedicate my arm, my back, my perfect body?

Objections.

The damsel simpers, an ice cream cone in her hand, Lolita sunglasses astride her nose, while Humpty Dumpty watches her from a few paces away, having made up his mind to.

Music!

The morning fanfare resounds.

Hurry!

Get up, suit up, take one's perch and one's prerogatives.

The news is heard.

— Three days to avoid war!

— Why three days? says astonished Lam, awakening.

74. — It's a mess, lui avait dit un autochtone à propos de la France ou du moins des manières dont les Français faisaient la queue.

Le même mot, ou presque, désignant donc la messe et le bordel.

— It's a mess, lui dit un autre Américain dans un aéroport, à Atlanta, cinq heures d'attente, un avion supprimé.

— Cancelled, répètent les employés.

Il ne les comprend pas, il doit sortir son dictionnaire.

Le mot dans sa mémoire, débarrassé de son contexte, est suspendu.

Il pense à cacheter et à prison, à cire, à candélabre, à Buñuel.

Il est un élément du paysage, familier, et pourtant il se tait.

Un homme vient lui demander si l'avion part pour Mexico.

Lam répond en anglais.

L'autre s'esclaffe, laisse son sac à dos.

À son retour, il tient des chips, qu'il offre à Lam, s'esclaffe encore.

Une vieille Asiatique ouvre son sac à main et y regarde longuement trois petites photos, mises sous cadre.

Quand elle y a puisé à suffisance, elle ferme son sac, jusqu'à une autre fois qui se produit bientôt.

74. *It's a mess!* a native had said to him regarding France, or at least the comportment of the French when standing in line.

Thus the same word, or nearly, designated the Mass and a shambles.

— *It's a mess*, another American says to him in an airport, in Atlanta, a five-hour wait, a flight cancelled.

— *Cancelled*, the employees repeat.

He doesn't understand them, he has to take out his dictionary.

Relieved of its context, the word stays suspended in his memory.

He thinks of cachet and of prison, of candle-wax, of candelabra, of Buñuel.

He is an element in the landscape, familiar, and yet he remains silent.

A man comes up to ask him if the plane is leaving for Mexico.

Lam answers in English.

The other man bursts out laughing, leaves his backpack.

When he returns, he is holding a bag of potato chips that he offers to Lam, bursts out laughing again.

An old Asian woman opens her handbag and gazes into it for a long time at three little framed photographs.

When she has drawn enough from them, she closes her bag, till another time, which will be soon.

75. Un jeune homme un peu gras porte un paquet dont il semble soucieux.

Il l'accroche à son siège, le décroche et le pose entre eux deux afin que Lam le voie.

C'est un ours en peluche.

Lam approuve sans comprendre le rapport entre l'homme et la bête.

Plus tard dans un journal il lui montre un article.

Lam lit AIDS, il opine.

— Oui je connais, partout, c'est grave, pas seulement en Amérique.

Il semble soulagé, lui montre la peluche qui pend sous leurs regards, cadeau pour un ami qui a la maladie.

Une très grosse dame donne la main à deux fillettes en robe blanche, chaussettes bien tirées, cheveux tressés et attachés par des rubans.

Ce sont des noires d'Amérique, des noires qui ne sont pas d'Afrique, qui sont nourries de hamburgers et de sodas.

À côté trois garçons, noirs aussi, magnifiques, venus de quel soleil on se demande, et depuis quand ?

On ne voit pas d'Indiens.

Dans la région des Fingerlakes, si on veut bien, on perçoit leur présence.

Ils ont laissé des noms aux paysages, aux tumulus qui sont des tombes.

75. A plump young man is holding a package that seems to preoccupy him.

He attaches it to his seat, detaches it, and puts it between the two of them so Lam can see.

It's a teddy bear.

Lam approves without understanding what connects the man to the animal.

Later he shows him an article in a newspaper.

Lam reads AIDS, he nods.

— Yes, I know, everywhere, it's serious, not only in America.

The young man seems relieved, shows him the stuffed animal that hangs beneath their gaze, a gift for a friend who has the illness.

A very fat lady holds two little girls by the hand, in white dresses, socks pulled up, their hair braided and tied with ribbons.

They are black Americans, blacks who are not from Africa, who are nourished on hamburgers and sodas.

Beside them three boys, black also, magnificent, come from beneath what sun, one asks oneself, and how long ago?

One doesn't see any Indians.

In the Finger Lakes region, if one cares, there are signs of their presence.

They've left names for the landscapes, for the tumuli that are tombs.

76. Un ami en montre un en passant, à côté d'un hangar.

Lam ne voit rien de remarquable, le sol un peu gonflé.

— Afin qu'on n'oublie pas, dit l'ami, libanais d'origine, qu'on ne supprime pas le cimetière, en construisant la route, exprès dessus.

« On n'imagine pas quelle violence. »

— L'exil, explique un autre, cette fois espagnol, c'est une pierre dans le coeur.

« C'est une épreuve, c'est effroyable.

« Ni ici, ni ailleurs. Je suis seul. »

Pourtant chacun est *nice*, tout comme les maisons, et loin des centres qui s'effondrent, qui sont déshabités.

Dans ce pays on aime l'isolement et la forêt.

L'espace.

Jamais organisé, sans référence, ni point de convergence.

Dilué.

Du moins pour Lam, qui cherche des repères, par exemple à savoir s'il se rapproche ou s'il s'éloigne.

Mais par rapport à quoi ?

76. A friend shows one of them to him in passing, beside a hangar.

Lam sees nothing remarkable, the earth slightly pushed up.

— So that they are not forgotten, says the friend, of Lebanese origin, so that they don't destroy the cemetery, building the highway, deliberately, over it.

"You can't imagine the violence."

— Exile, explains another, Spanish this time, is a stone in the heart.

"It's an ordeal, it's frightful.

"Neither here, nor elsewhere. I am alone."

Yet everyone is *nice*, just like the houses, and far from the town centers, which are collapsing, which are uninhabited.

In this country they like isolation and the forest.

Space.

Never organized, without points of reference or points of convergence.

Diluted.

Or so it seems to Lam, who is looking for landmarks, to know for example if he is coming closer or going farther away.

But in reference to what?

77. Lawrence Ferlinghetti emmène Lam en promenade.

Il a placé son chien entre eux, pour éviter que les passants ne le bousculent.

Aveugle et blanc comme la tête du poète.

— J'espère, dit-il, en remuant ses lèvres, humides et roses, et attachant le chien, que cette fois je ne l'oublierai pas toute la nuit.

Lam fait un rêve.

Il est dans un palais.

Les murs sont des étoffes et les appartements s'emplissent d'eau.

Cependant que les femmes disparaissent, derrière des paravents, les hommes se consultent.

Les parois sont mouillées par la mer.

En se penchant par les fenêtres il aperçoit la rade, d'autres palais semblables, éclairés par le jour déclinant.

— Je crois que je confonds, que je suis à Venise, dans un rêve de peinture.

Tournée vers le Seneca Lake, la Française a un air égaré.

— Ici, ni barrières, ni haies.

« En l'absence de limites, le regard ne peut pas s'arrêter. »

77. Lawrence Ferlinghetti takes Lam for a walk.

He has placed his dog between them so that people passing won't bump into him.

Blind and white like the poet's head.

— I hope, he says, moving his lips, damp and pink, and tying up the dog, that this time I won't forget about him all night long.

Lam has a dream.

He is in a palace.

The walls are made of fabric and the apartments are filling up with water.

While the women disappear, behind screens, the men confer.

The partitions are soaked with sea-water.

Leaning out the window, he sees the harbor, similar palaces, lit by the fading daylight.

— I think that I'm confusing things, that I'm in Venice, in a dream about a painting.

Turned toward Seneca Lake, the Frenchwoman looks distraught.

— No fences here, and no hedges.

"Lacking limits, the gaze has nowhere to stop."

78. Petite danse

78. Little Dance

79. Les vents insistent.

Ils sont dits vents constants. Tu observes.

Depuis les chambres, depuis les tentes, ou sur les routes.

Les vents vont vite.

Contrairement à nous, les vents vont vite.

Soit ils tournent, soit ils creusent.

Mais toujours ils s'échauffent, ils soulèvent.

Ils sont ailleurs et toujours là, dans nos cheveux, sur nos figures.

Tu aimerais qu'ils cessent. Tu t'accroches pour ne pas leur céder.

Mais ils sifflent.

Tu ne peux pas ne pas entendre. Être dehors.

Dehors d'eux et du sable.

L'émotion est trop forte. Tu peux tomber.

Faire une tache.

79. The winds insist.
They are called constant winds. You observe.
From within rooms, from tents, or on the roads.
The winds move quickly.
Unlike us, the winds move quickly.
Either they turn or they dig.
But they continue to heat up, they rise.
They are always there, in our hair, on our faces.
You would like them to stop. You hang on so as not to give in to them.
But they whistle.
You cannot not hear them. Be beyond.
Beyond them, beyond the sand.
The feeling is too strong. You might fall.
Make a stain.

80. Tu parcours le pays à cheval. Tu ne vois rien que ce qui vole.

L'horizon effacé, le ciel dessous, dessous les pieds, le sable jaune.

C'est la couleur de l'incendie, pense l'enfant.

Elle veut dire : de l'enfer.

De l'Azeffal à l'Amsaga, d'Inchiti à Targa jusqu'à Boutilimit, rien n'est possible hormis durer.

Tenter la ligne droite. Rester debout. Rester ouvert, pour observer.

Compter.

Tant de cailloux, de tessons et de roches.

Enumérer.

19 novembre. Départ à l'aube. Le sable est plat, amoncelé ou ondulé. Une vipère à cornes siffle. En fin de jour marche au désert.

23 novembre. Arrivée à Rayân, où sont des sources, des végétaux.

26 novembre. Petits tertres de sable. Plaine déserte nommée Garderamak.

28 novembre. Tout le jour sol uni. Sur le soir, longues dunes. Cul-de-sac dans les sables nommé Abougarah.

29 novembre. Troncs d'arbres pétrifiés, sources d'eau douce et végétaux, plaine de sable, nommée el-Ma-Assâs.

80. You cross the country on horseback. All you can see is what flies.

The horizon effaced, the sky below, below your feet, the yellow sand.

It's the color of fire, thinks the child.

She means: of hell.

From the Azeffal to the Amsaga, from Inchiti to Targa all the way to Boutlimit, nothing is possible but enduring.

Risking the direct route. Staying upright. Staying alert, to observe.

To count.

So many pebbles, shards of clay and rocks.

To enumerate.

November 19. Departure at dawn. The sand is flat, banked up or in ripples. A horned serpent whistles. A walk in the desert at nightfall.

November 23. Arrival at Rayân, where there are water sources, plants.

November 26. Little mounds of sand. A deserted plain, called Garderamak.

November 28. The soil all one color all day. Towards evening, long dunes. A dead end in the sand, called Abougarah.

November 29. Petrified tree trunks, freshwater sources and plants, a plain of sand, called el-Ma-Assâs.

81. Tu notes.
Vent fort.
Vent fort.
Vent fort.
Tu crois avoir tout dit.
Tu notes encore.
Gelée blanche dans la nuit.
Grains de pluie à neuf heures du matin.
Grains de pluie à onze heures du matin.
Grains de pluie à midi.
Le vent se lève avec violence, depuis le nord.
Dans la nuit il devient presque calme.
Tout le jour, vent couvert.
Tout le mois vent violent.

81. You note.
Strong wind.
Strong wind.
Strong wind.
You think you've said everything.
You note again.
White frost during the night.
Drops of rain at nine in the morning.
Drops of rain at eleven in the morning.
Drops of rain at noon.
The wind rises violently, from the north.
During the night, it becomes almost calm.
All day long, muffled wind.
All month long, violent wind.

82. Tu agis sans y croire.

D'ailleurs tu oublies tout.

T'es-tu levée, lavée ?

T'es-tu battue pour échapper ?

Tu as des jupes autour des jambes et un chapeau à larges bords, pour sortir de chez toi.

Mais vent très fort, sable jaune, chaque jour.

Quelques rapaces noirs.

Un compagnon silencieux.

Peut-être a-t-il du bon ?

Allez savoir.

Tu ne le quittes pas.

Tu essaies de ne pas le quitter.

Car souvent il s'en va.

Tu l'attends.

82. You act without believing in it.

Besides, you forget everything.

Did you get up, wash?

Did you struggle to escape?

You have skirts around your legs and a wide-brimmed hat, to go outdoors.

But strong wind, yellow sand, every day.

A few black raptors.

A silent companion.

Perhaps he has his good points?

Go find out!

You don't leave him.

You try not to leave him.

Because he often leaves.

You wait for him.

83. Tu ne veux pas l'attendre.

Tu te crois assez forte.

Tu t'en vas seule.

Parfois, tu suis un grimacier, qui en prend l'habitude.

Tu fais des randonnées.

Quand tu reviens tu as perdu.

Tu as perdu jusqu'à l'idée d'apaisement.

Tu crois qu'il est ailleurs de toi.

Qu'il faut l'aller chercher.

Dans l'Orient, sur la mer.

Entre les mains d'un autre.

Tu pars encore. Rien sur la rive.

Tu ne pars plus. Le vent bouge, envahit les terrasses.

Tu te mets à sécher, tu reviens à la vie, toujours prête.

83. You don't want to wait for him.

You think you're strong enough yourself.

You go off alone.

Sometimes you follow a hypocrite, who gets used to it.

You go for hikes.

When you come back, you've lost.

You've lost even the idea of reassurance.

You think it's somewhere beyond you.

That you must go in search of it.

In the Orient, on the sea.

In someone else's hands.

You set off once more. Nothing on the riverbank.

You don't leave again. The wind moves, invades the terraces.

You set yourself out to dry, you come back to life, always ready.

84. Les oiseaux manquent.

Ils manquent de place, de ciel.

Ils n'ont pas où voler.

Tu as les yeux fermés et tu les rêves.

Tu vois le ciel, dans sa couleur des jours sans vent, sa couleur qu'on dit bleue.

La maladie du ciel existe, pense l'enfant.

Tu les vois dans le ciel.

Sans raison apparente, ils quittent leur pays, près du pôle nord.

Leur trajet par les terres et les mers est précis.

Le Danube, la mer Noire, le Bosphore, et le Nil. L'Éthiopie maintenant.

Et le désert Kalahari, près du Pôle Sud.

Ou la Nouvelle Écosse, le Gulf Stream, la Guyane, le Brésil. Le Chili maintenant.

Et la Patagonie.

Ou l'Alaska, les îles Hawaii, Nouvelle-Zélande, Nouvelle-Guinée. Et l'Australie.

84. The birds are missing.

They don't have enough space, enough sky.

They have nowhere to fly.

You have your eyes closed and you dream them.

You see the sky, in its color of windless days, its color called blue.

The sickness of the sky exists, thinks the child.

You see them in the sky.

With no apparent reason, they leave their territory, near the North Pole.

Their route across land and sea is exact.

The Danube, the Black Sea, the Bosphorus and the Nile. Now Ethiopia.

And the Kalahari Desert, near the South Pole.

Or Nova Scotia, the Gulf Stream. Guinea, Brazil. Now Chile.

And Patagonia.

Or Alaska, the Hawaiian Islands, New Zealand, New Guinea. And Australia.

85. Gelée blanche et vent fort.
Tout le mois vent brûlant.
L'enfant dit :
— Je vais voir mon amie catalane.
« Je me dépêche.
« Trop souvent je la manque.
« Trop souvent elle s'absente.
« Je me couche sur elle.
« Un lit de feuilles sèches.
« C'est odorant, ça craque.
« Quand j'ai fini elle dit :
« C'est beau comme une maison.
« Chaque fois dit : c'est beau comme une maison.
« Je me mets à chanter à tue-tête. »

85. White frost and strong wind.
Burning wind all month long.
The child says:
— I go to see my Catalan friend.
"I hurry.
"Too often, I just miss her.
"Too often, she's gone away.
"I lie down on top of her.
"A bed of dry leaves.
"It's fragrant, it crackles.
"When I'm finished, she says:
"It's beautiful, like a house.
"Every time, says: it's beautiful like a house.
"I begin to sing at the top of my lungs."

86. Les mots sont des maisons.

Vent violent et oiseaux.

L'enfant les pèse, les pose.

Petite pluie de nuit.

L'enfant les met dans sa chaleur.

Temps couvert chaque jour.

Les mots n'ont rien à dire.

Quelle douceur, pense l'enfant.

Quand un grand crie, un plus petit accourt, la langue hors de la bouche. Ce qu'il appelle sa compassion.

— Du sens, du sens ! demande-t-on de tous côtés.

L'enfant soupire. Le grand dégoût.

— Tu m'aimes ? demande la vie.

— Je reviendrai, répond l'enfant avec sagesse.

Et à présent « petite danse dans le canon ».

86. Words are houses.
Violent wind and birds.
The child weighs them, sets them down.
Little nocturnal rain.
The child shelters them in his body heat.
Skies overcast every day.
The words have nothing to say.
Such sweetness, thinks the child.
When a big one cries out, a little one runs to him, tongue hanging out. What he calls his compassion.
— Some sense! Some sense! they cry out from all sides.
The child sighs. Great weariness.
— Do you love me? life asks.
— I'll come back, the child answers sensibly.
And now "a little dance in the cannon's mouth."

87. Spécial rétable.

Ce qu'indique le carton griffonné au-dessus de l'entrée.

Ou de l'image, comme on voudra.

Les baladins sont sur la place. Par derrière, les lumières des maisons.

Ils sont vêtus de rouge, de bleu, de jaune.

Tiennent en laisse un singe, un perroquet, et un ballon.

— C'est un fragment, dit l'homme, le héros de la pièce.

« Je dois encore y travailler.

« Y travailler beaucoup.

« Ou le jeter.

« Qu'en pensez-vous ? »

Il s'adresse au public.

Il soupire :

— Si difficile de toucher juste !

87. Altarpiece special.

That's what's on the scribbled cardboard above the entrance.

Or above the image, if you prefer.

The traveling players are in the square. Behind them, lights in houses.

They are dressed in red, in blue, in yellow.

Holding a leashed monkey, a parakeet, and a balloon.

— It's only an excerpt, says the man, the hero of the play.

"I still have to work on it.

"Work on it quite a bit.

"Or ditch it.

"What do you think?"

He's talking to the audience.

He sighs:

— It's so hard to hit the right note!

88. — J'avais un fils, dit-il.

« J'avais une fille. »

Pendant ce temps la baladine en robe bleue, heureuse presque.

— J'ai vu, dit le héros.

« O mon coeur plein de larmes.

« J'ai vu mon coeur en aparté, il contenait. Il contenait cela, qui me brûlait.

« Au milieu de la messe je brisai ma guitare.

« Mais à présent je parle, je danse à ma façon bizarre. »

C'est le moment des choses sèches.

C'est la grande assemblée des oiseaux à l'automne.

L'allégresse a des mots inutiles.

Tandis que la tristesse existe, sons dépêchés, sur le visage de la Dame.

Dans l'air, nulle ombre, juste des traits.

L'eau toute blanche dort.

88. — I had a son, he says.

"I had a daughter."

All this time, the actress, in a blue dress, almost happy.

— I saw, says the hero.

"O my heart, full of tears.

"I took my heart aside, it contained. It contained something that burned me.

"In the midst of the mass, I broke my guitar.

"Now I speak, now I dance, in my own odd way."

It was the moment of dry things.

It was the great gathering of the birds in autumn.

Joy has words, but useless ones.

So long as sorrow exists, sounds dispatched, on the face of the Lady.

In the air, not a shadow, only features.

The water, in all its whiteness, sleeps.

89. Certains sont japonais

89. Some of Them Are Japanese

90. À l'automne ils s'envolent.

Ils gagnent l'équateur, ils pénètrent si loin qu'ils n'ont rien à manger.

Ils reviennent si tôt qu'ils ont froid et qu'ils meurent.

Qu'ils ont faim et qu'ils meurent.

Ils meurent deux fois, dix fois.

Certains sont sédentaires et certains migrateurs.

Leurs ailes courtes volent mal.

Certains sont japonais.

Ils volent deux milles, cinq milles, dix milles. Sans se poser.

Que cherchent-ils ? On cherche.

Leur chemin est celui des glaciers.

Au moment du départ, l'air est troublé mais vide.

Même en cage ils s'agitent.

90. In the autumn, they fly off.

They reach the equator, they venture so far that they have nothing to eat.

They come back so soon that they are cold and they die.

That they are hungry and they die.

They die twice, ten times.

Some of them are sedentary and some are migrants.

Their short wings are bad for flying.

Some of them are Japanese.

They fly two miles, five miles, ten miles. Without landing.

What are they looking for? We look for it.

Their path is the way of the glaciers.

At the moment of departure, the air is troubled, but empty.

Even in cages, they keep moving.

91. Vivent dix ans, vingt ans, trente ans.

Ne s'assoient pas. Ne dorment pas non plus.

Leurs ailes manquent de mains.

Leur bouche manque de dents.

Leur ventre de vessie.

Réduit à un cloaque.

De cloaque à cloaque ils copulent.

Ainsi sont-ils légers.

Légèreté les mène.

Les mène loin et haut.

Quand ils sont abattus, si leurs poumons sont pleins de sang, ils respirent par les os de leurs ailes.

Prolongent leur vie d'autant.

Leur souffrance d'autant.

La mort quand même vient.

91. Live for ten years, twenty years, thirty years.
Don't sit down. Don't sleep, either.
Their wings lack hands.
Their mouths lack teeth.
Their pelvises lack a bladder.
Reduced to a cloaca.
Cloaca to cloaca, they copulate.
Thus they are light.
Lightness leads them.
Leads them farther and higher.
When they are exhausted, if their lungs are full of blood, they breathe through the bones of their wings.
Prolong their lives that way.
Their suffering that way.
Death comes nonetheless.

92. Tous ne sont pas en l'air.

Pas obligés.

Certains creusent des trous, certains nagent, certains grimpent.

Ne quittent pas leur arbre ou seulement pour leur toilette.

Qui dure, qui dure.

Le plus souvent furent massacrés.

Autrefois ils étaient abondants.

Obscurcissaient le ciel.

Mais l'orage vient d'en bas, au contraire des croyances.

L'orage les a exterminés, vendus en vrac sur les marchés, peau morte, viande inutile.

Les a jetés aux porcs, transformés en engrais.

On les nommait comment déjà ?

Paradisiers ?

92. All of them aren't in the air.

Not obliged to be.

Some of them dig holes, some swim, some climb.

Never leave their trees, or only for grooming.

Which goes on, and on.

Were usually massacred.

Once they were abundant.

Darkened the sky.

But the storm came from below, despite what was believed.

The storm exterminated them, sold wholesale on the marketplace, dead skin, useless meat.

Threw them to the pigs, used them for fertilizer.

What were they called again?

Birds of paradise?

93. Ils ont le don du chant à condition d'apprendre.

Chanter s'apprend comme le reste.

Comme marcher au bout du monde.

Lever les yeux.

Offrir ses mains.

S'asseoir devant la porte, tête inclinée.

Par la fenêtre ouverte, regarder ce qui brille, qui est derrière les arbres, l'ombre qui vient avec le soir.

Partir.

Allez, allez !

Ils ont de la mémoire.

Par exemple, quand la porte est trop grande, quand un rêve les tracasse, que le soleil monte et descend, ils comprennent leur bonheur.

Ils restent, ils n'ont pas peur.

Moins gris que de coutume.

93. They have the gift of song provided that they learn.
Singing is learned like anything else.
Like walking to the end of the world.
Lifting up one's eyes.
Offering one's hands.
Sitting down in front of the door, head bent.
Out the open window, looking at what burns, what is beyond the trees, the shadow that comes with the evening.
Leaving.
Go on, go on!
They have memory.
For example, when the door is too large, when a dream worries them, when the sun rises and sets, they understand their happiness.
They stay, they are not afraid.
Less gray than usual.

94. Lors des massacres, certains furent épargnés.

L'or manquait à leur cou.

Plus tard, quand ils chantèrent, quand ils parlèrent avec les mots des anciens maîtres, des maîtres massacrés, nul ne comprit.

La langue aussi avait été exterminée.

Comme quoi, le meilleur chant ne suffit pas.

Pour garder le terrain, la femelle.

Il faut aussi voler la nuit.

Ne jamais retourner même après des années, sur un lieu de danger.

Continuer autrement et ailleurs.

Etre meilleur chanteur, meilleur lutteur.

Créer sans cesse des variations.

Marcher dans les couleurs qui changent, autour du cercle merveilleux.

Marquer le sol.

Dessiner un carré à son nombre.

94. During the massacres, some of them were spared.

They didn't have enough gold on their necks.

Later, when they sang, when they spoke in the words of their former leaders, of their slaughtered leaders, no one understood them.

Their language too had been exterminated.

This proves that even the best singing does not suffice.

To hold your territory, your female.

It's also necessary to fly at night.

Never to return, even years later, to a dangerous spot.

To continue otherwise and elsewhere.

To be a better singer, a better fighter.

To create constant variations.

To walk amidst changing colors, around the miraculous circle.

To mark the earth.

To draw a square with one's own number.

95. On dit.

Ils ne savent ni parler ni chanter.

Ils répètent.

Les hommes aussi répètent, bien qu'ils aient deux cerveaux.

Les hommes sont des diables à qui manquent l'atmosphère, le courage, la lueur.

On dit.

Ils sont farceurs.

Oiseaux humains.

Ils chantent faux exprès, afin qu'on les imite, croyant bien faire.

Ou bien.

Ils annoncent un danger, l'épervier.

Afin qu'on prenne peur.

Dès qu'on s'enfuit ils rient.

Plissent les yeux et voient : à présent le jour neige.

95. It's said.

They don't know either how to speak or how to sing.

They repeat.

Men repeat as well, even though they have two brains.

Men are devils who lack ambiance, color, light.

It's said.

That they are jokers.

Human birds.

They sing off-key deliberately, to be imitated, so that those who imitate them will think they're singing true.

Or perhaps.

They announce a danger, the sparrowhawk.

To frighten those who hear them.

As soon as they've fled, they laugh.

Wrinkle their eyes and see: right now it's snowing.

96. Certains sont jardiniers, ils construisent des tonnelles qu'ils décorent.

De fleurs, de mousse, de coquillages. De cadeaux pour aimer.

La femelle a le droit de refuser l'hommage, de s'envoler de la balustre.

Les spectateurs sont sur les branches.

Au milieu sur la scène, un acteur fait semblant de se battre.

Avec un scorpion mort ou un mille-pattes.

L'acteur n'est pas acteur, il est un homme qui veut séduire. La femelle est entrée dans le rang, elle est parmi les spectateurs.

Le mâle la prend et la féconde.

Quand elle couve, il l'emmure.

Pendant des jours elle est captive, ses plumes tombent, elle s'en sert de coussins.

Le mâle la nourrit.

Quand elle sort il n'a plus que la peau sur les os.

96. Some of them are gardeners, they construct arbors that they decorate.

With flowers, with moss, with shells. Love-gifts.

The female has the right to refuse this homage, to fly off the balustrade.

The audience sits in the branches.

At the center of the stage, an actor pretends to beat himself.

With a dead scorpion or a millipede.

The actor isn't an actor, he's a man bent on seduction. The female has taken her place in one row, she is among the spectators.

The male takes her and fecundates her.

While she's sitting on the eggs, he walls her up.

During the days of her captivity, her feathers fall out, she uses them as cushions.

The male feeds her.

When she emerges, he's nothing but skin and bones.

97. Bateleur couronné.
Sa tête est grise.
Sa nuque rousse.
Il bourdonne, sentinelle.
Il est flambé, masqué, pointé.
Les narines emplumées.
Le bec ouvert et la queue noire.
Ses joues sont grises.
Il aboie, il combat, arlequin.
Il est doré, gracile.
Huppé, cendré, féroce.
Intermédiaire.
Ravisseur et variable.
Martial et montagnard.

97. Crowned acrobat.
His head is gray.
The back of his neck, russet.
He hums, standing guard.
He is flaming, masked, spotted.
Feathered nostrils.
An open beak and a black tail.
His cheeks are gray.
He barks, he battles, harlequin.
He is gilded, slender.
Crested, ashen, ferocious.
Go-between.
Kidnapper and changeable.
Military and mountain-dweller.

98. Il habite les rochers, le désert, les marais.

Sa nuque est bleue.

Son ventre est blanc.

Sa nuque est jaune.

Il est terne, à dos vert.

Il est veuf, à deux taches.

On le dit jacobin, capucin, solitaire.

Épiscopal.

On le dit polyglotte, garde-boeuf, à longs brins.

Soyeux du Sénégal.

Noir de Fernando Po.

Vêtu de cape jaune.

À lunettes orientales.

Sans parler du croupion tricolore.

98. He inhabits the rocks, the desert, the swamps.
The nape of his neck is blue.
His belly is white.
The nape of his neck is yellow.
He is dull, with a green back.
He is a widower, with two colored spots.
He's said to be a Jacobin, a Capuchin, a hermit.
Episcopal.
He's said to be polyglot, a cattle egret, with long strands.
Silky from Senegal.
Black from Fernando Po.
Dressed in a yellow cape.
With oriental glasses.
Not to mention the tricolor rump.

99. L'enfant a pris les mots, les oiseaux et les vents.

Il en a fait cent parts.

Je mets tout de ma vie, j'adore ça.

Baiser la nuit, son bord, c'est ma cuisine.

Il boit du noir en traits, il voit des transparences.

Comme on dit, l'autre monde.

Du noir en pluie, du blanc tassé.

Pelures et plumes.

Des ombres quelquefois, des tentations.

Des coups mouillés derrière la vitre.

Des cernes sous le clair.

Derrière les volets clos, la lumière extérieure.

Les couleurs sans couleurs, tôt lavées, du désert, où l'enfant se promène entre les rochers blancs.

Roi des cents cavaliers.

99. The child has taken the words, the birds, the winds.
He has divided them into a hundred sections.
I put in every part of my life. I love that.
To kiss the night, its edges, that's my kitchen.
He drinks darkness in gulps, he sees clarities.
As they say, the other world.
Black rains down, strong-brewed white.
Peelings and feathers.
Shadows sometimes, and temptations.
Damp blows behind the windowpane.
Shadow-rings in daylight.
Behind the closed shutters, outdoor light.
The desert's colorless colors soon washed-out, where the child walks among white rocks.
King of a hundred horsemen.

100. Avec des citations de

Thomas Stearns Eliot (3), Paul Claudel (3), Marina Tsvetaeva (4, 5),

Fedor Dostoievsky (10), Pascal Mougin, photographe (11),

Moallaca de Harith (19, 44), Paul Blackburn (20), Marie-Louise Fleischer (22),

Le Tasse (28), Mathieu Bénézet (30), Robert Musil (31, 66), Rosamond Lehmann (37),

Gaston Planet, peintre (37 à 40), Italo Svevo (44), François Dilasser, peintre (57 à 66),

Tristan Tzara (78, 86).

Et des incitations de

Véronique Lossky (4, 5) pour les colloques : « Un chant de vie », 1992, « Marina Tsvetaeva et la France », 2000,

Patrick Kéchichian (7, 8) pour *Le Monde*, « Poésies vivantes d'aujourd'hui »,

Michel Roudier (37 à 40) pour le catalogue de l'exposition à l'Abbaye-aux-Dames, Saintes, 1997,

Jacques Darras (67 à 73), pour *In'hui*, 1998,

Dominique Moncond'huy (57 à 66) pour *La Licorne*, Faculté des Lettres de l'Université de Poitiers, 1998.

100. With quotations from

T. S. Eliot (3), Paul Claudel (3), Marina Tsvetaeva (4, 5);

Fyodor Dostoevsky (10), Pascal Mougin, photographer (11);

Moallaca de Harith (19, 44), Paul Blackburn (20), Marie-Louise Fleischer (22);

Torquato Tasso (28), Mathieu Bénézet (30), Robert Musil (31, 66), Rosamond Lehmann (37);

Gaston Planet, painter (37 to 40), Italo Svevo (44), François Dilasser, painter (57 to 66);

Tristan Tzara (78, 86).

And incitements from

Véronique Lossky (4, 5) for organizing the conferences: "A song of life," 1992, "Marina Tsvetaeva and France," 2000;

Patrick Kéchichian (7, 8) for his article in *Le Monde*, "Living Poetries Today," summer 1998;

Michel Roudier (37 to 40) for the catalogue of the exhibition at L'Abbaye-aux-Dames, Saintes, 1997;

Jacques Darras (67 to 73) for *InHui*, 1998;

Dominique Moncond'huy (57 to 66) for *The Unicorn*, School of the Arts, University of Poitiers, 1998.